CAMBRIDGE
UNIVERSITY PRESS

CAMBRIDGE
Primary Science

Teacher's Resource 4

Fiona Baxter & Liz Dilley

CAMBRIDGE
UNIVERSITY PRESS

Shaftesbury Road, Cambridge CB2 8EA, United Kingdom

One Liberty Plaza, 20th Floor, New York, NY 10006, USA

477 Williamstown Road, Port Melbourne, VIC 3207, Australia

314–321, 3rd Floor, Plot 3, Splendor Forum, Jasola District Centre, New Delhi – 110025, India

103 Penang Road, #05–06/07, Visioncrest Commercial, Singapore 238467

Cambridge University Press is part of the University of Cambridge.

It furthers the University's mission by disseminating knowledge in the pursuit of education, learning and research at the highest international levels of excellence.

www.cambridge.org
Information on this title: www.cambridge.org/9781108785280

© Cambridge University Press & Assessment 2021

First published 2014
Second edition 2021

20 19 18 17 16 15 14 13 12 11 10 9 8 7 6 5

Printed in Poland by Opolgraf

A catalogue record for this publication is available from the British Library

ISBN 978-1-108-78528-0 Paperback with Digital access

Cambridge University Press has no responsibility for the persistence or accuracy of URLs for external or third-party internet websites referred to in this publication, and does not guarantee that any content on such websites is, or will remain, accurate or appropriate. Information regarding prices, travel timetables, and other factual information given in this work is correct at the time of first printing but Cambridge University Press does not guarantee the accuracy of such information thereafter.

Cambridge International copyright material in this publication is reproduced under licence and remains the intellectual property of Cambridge Assessment International Education.

Test-style questions [and sample answers] have been written by the authors. In Cambridge Checkpoint tests or Cambridge Progression tests, the way marks are awarded may be different. References to assessment and/or assessment preparation are the publisher's interpretation of the curriculum framework requirements and may not fully reflect the approach of Cambridge Assessment International Education.

Third-party websites and resources referred to in this publication have not been endorsed by Cambridge Assessment International Education.

NOTICE TO TEACHERS IN THE UK

It is illegal to reproduce any part of this work in material form (including photocopying and electronic storage) except under the following circumstances:

(i) where you are abiding by a licence granted to your school or institution by the Copyright Licensing Agency;

(ii) where no such licence exists, or where you wish to exceed the terms of a licence, and you have gained the written permission of Cambridge University Press;

(iii) where you are allowed to reproduce without permission under the provisions of Chapter 3 of the Copyright, Designs and Patents Act 1988, which covers, for example, the reproduction of short passages within certain types of educational anthology and reproduction for the purposes of setting examination questions.

> Contents

Introduction   v

Acknowledgements   vi

About the authors   vii

How to use this series   viii

How to use this Teacher's Resource   x

About the curriculum framework   xv

About the assessment   xv

Approaches to learning and teaching   xvi

Setting up for success   xviii

Teaching notes

1   Living things   2

2   Energy   26

3   Materials   44

4   Earth and its habitats   66

5   Light   83

6   Electricity   107

Glossary   131

Digital resources

The following items are available on Cambridge GO. For more information on how to access and use your digital resource, please see inside front cover.

Active learning

Assessment for Learning

Developing learner language skills

Differentiation

Improving learning through questioning

Language awareness

Metacognition

Skills for Life

Letter for parents – Introducing the Cambridge Primary resources

Lesson plan template and examples of completed lesson plans

Curriculum framework correlation

Scheme of work

Diagnostic check and answers

Mid-point test and answers

End-of-year test and answers

Answers to Learner's Book questions

Answers to Workbook questions

Glossary

You can download the following resources for each unit:

Differentiated worksheets and answers

Language worksheets and answers

Resource sheets

End-of-unit tests and answers

> Introduction

Welcome to the new edition of our Cambridge Primary Science series.

Since its launch, the series has been used by teachers and learners in over 100 countries for teaching the Cambridge Primary Science curriculum framework.

This exciting new edition has been designed by talking to Primary Science teachers all over the world. We have worked hard to understand your needs and challenges, and then carefully designed and tested the best ways of meeting them.

As a result of this research, we've made some important changes to the series. This Teacher's Resource has been carefully redesigned to make it easier for you to plan and teach the course.

The series still has extensive digital and online support, including Digital Classroom, which lets you share books with your class and play videos and audio. This Teacher's Resource also offers additional materials available to download from Cambridge GO. (For more information on how to access and use your digital resource, please see inside front cover.)

The series uses the most successful teaching pedagogies like active learning and metacognition and this Teacher's Resource gives you full guidance on how to integrate them into your classroom.

Formative assessment opportunities help you to get to know your learners better, with clear learning intentions and success criteria, as well as an array of assessment techniques, including advice on self and peer assessment.

Clear, consistent differentiation ensures that all learners are able to progress in the course with tiered activities, differentiated worksheets and advice about supporting learners' different needs.

All our resources are written for teachers and learners who use English as a second or additional language. They help learners build core English skills with vocabulary and grammar support, as well as additional language worksheets.

We hope you enjoy using this course.

Eddie Rippeth

Head of Primary and Lower Secondary Publishing, Cambridge University Press

> Acknowledgements

Thanks to the following for permission to reproduce images:

Cover illustration by Omar Aranda (Beehive Illustration); *within worksheets* Wayne Eastep/Getty Images, Yamoto_Sardi/Getty Images; Planet Observer/Universal Images Group/Getty Images

> About the authors

Fiona Baxter

Fiona Baxter has been involved in Science education for over 25 years and has many years of Science teaching experience. In recent years her main focus has been on developing learning materials for both primary and secondary school curricula. One of Fiona's areas of interest in Science education is making science more accessible to both teachers and learners, particularly in developing countries, through the use of low cost, everyday materials for practical work. She also feels strongly about the inclusion of girls in Science activities in the classroom and the workplace.

Fiona believes that using the Cambridge Primary Science series will help learners to build a strong conceptual foundation for further studies in Science, while at the same time making the learning experience engaging and fun.

Liz Dilley

Liz was born and educated in London and did a BSc and post graduate diploma in Education at the University of Bristol.

Shortly after university she moved to South Africa, where she taught for several years before training as a second-language English writer. This led to a variety of experiences in teacher training, adult education and writing for school-aged learners.

From the mid-1990s Liz began to focus more on writing textbooks for Life Sciences, Physical Science and Social Sciences. She wrote textbooks for the new Namibian curriculum and later the new South African curriculum – about 200 titles in total.

In 2012–2016 she co-authored the Cambridge Primary Science Series and is now a co-author of the new series.

Liz lives in Cape Town, South Africa, with her husband and family. She enjoys hiking, boating and travelling to interesting places.

> How to use this series

The Learner's Book is designed for students to use in class with guidance from the teacher. It contains six units which offer complete coverage of the curriculum framework. A variety of investigations, activities, questions and images motivate students and help them to develop the necessary scientific skills. Each unit contains opportunities for formative assessment, differentiation and reflection so you can support your learners' needs and help them progress.

The Teacher's Resource is the foundation of this series and you'll find everything you need to deliver the course in here, including suggestions for differentiation, formative assessment and language support, teaching ideas, answers, unit and progress tests and extra worksheets. Each Teacher's Resource includes:

- A print book with detailed teaching notes for each topic
- Digital Access with all the material from the book in digital form plus editable planning documents, extra guidance, worksheets and more

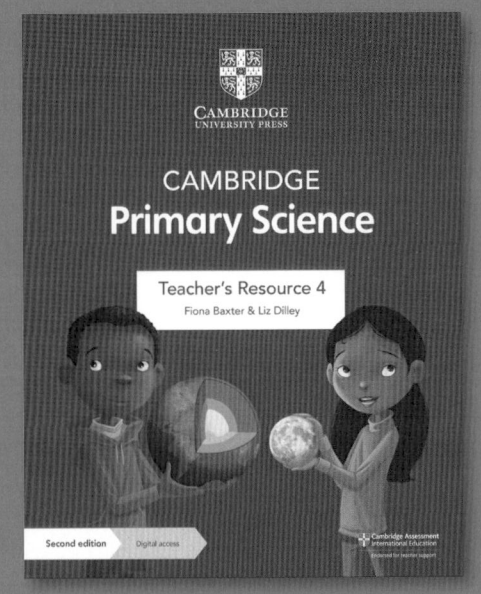

The skills-focused write-in Workbook provides further practice of all the topics in the Learner's Book and is ideal for use in class or as homework. A three-tier, scaffolded approach to skills development promotes visible progress and enables independent learning, ensuring that every learner is supported.

Digital Classroom includes digital versions of the Learner's Book and Workbook, complete with pop-up answers, and is designed for teachers to use at the front of class. Easily share the books with the whole class on your whiteboard, zoom in, highlight and annotate text, and get your learners talking with videos, images and interactive activities.

A letter to parents, explaining the course, is available to download from Cambridge GO (as part of this Teacher's Resource).

> How to use this Teacher's Resource

This Teacher's Resource contains both general guidance and teaching notes that help you to deliver the content in our Cambridge Primary Science resources. Some of the material is provided as downloadable files, available on **Cambridge GO**. (For more information about how to access and use your digital resource, please see inside front cover.) See the Contents page for details of all the material available to you, both in this book and through Cambridge GO.

Teaching notes

This book provides **teaching notes** for each unit of the Learner's Book and Workbook. Each set of teaching notes contains the following features to help you deliver the unit.

The **Unit plan** summarises the topics covered in the unit, including the number of learning hours recommended for the topic, an outline of the learning content and the Cambridge resources that can be used to deliver the topic.

Topic	Approximate number of learning hours	Outline of learning content	Resources
1.2 Why we need a skeleton	2	Functions of the skeleton Measure length of bones, record data in a table	**Learner's Book:** Think like a scientist: Measuring bone lengths **Workbook:** Topic 1.2 ⬇ Worksheets 1.2A, 1.2B and 1.2C **Digital Classroom:** Song – Some body

The **Background knowledge** feature explains prior knowledge required to access the unit and gives suggestions for addressing any gaps in your learners' prior knowledge.

Learners' prior knowledge can be informally assessed through the **Getting started** feature in the Learner's Book.

The **Teaching skills focus** feature covers a teaching skill and suggests how to implement it in the unit.

BACKGROUND KNOWLEDGE

The skeleton is the structure inside our body that is made up of bones. The main functions of the skeleton are to provide a frame that supports the body; to protect internal organs such as the heart, lungs and brain; and to allow movement. The bones of the skeleton also grow, which allows us to grow.

TEACHING SKILLS FOCUS

Active learning

Active learning is a form of learning in which learners become more directly involved in the learning process. Younger learners, in particular, find it difficult to listen and concentrate for more than about five minutes at a time if they are not actively doing something.

Reflecting the Learner's Book, each unit consists of multiple sections. A section covers a learning topic.

At the start of each section, the **Learning plan** table includes the learning objectives, learning intentions and success criteria that are covered in the section.

It can be helpful to share learning intentions and success criteria with your learners at the start of a lesson so that they can begin to take responsibility for their own learning

LEARNING PLAN

Learning objectives	Learning intentions	Success criteria
4Bs.01 Identify some of the important bones in the human body (limited to skull, jaw, rib cage, hip, spine, leg bones and arm bones).	• To be able to name some of the bones in our body. To be able to point out where some of the main bones are found in our body.	• Learners can identify the skull, jaw, spine, rib cage, hip, arm bones and leg bones.

There are often **common misconceptions** associated with particular learning topics. These are listed, along with suggestions for identifying evidence of the misconceptions in your class and suggestions for how to overcome them.

Misconception	How to identify	How to overcome
Bones are not living.	Ask learners to describe bones. Are they living or non-living?	Ask learners if their bones are the same size now as when they were babies. The answer is no, which shows that bones grow. Learners should recall from Stage 3 that growth is a life process.

For each topic, there is a selection of **starter ideas**, **main teaching ideas** and **plenary ideas**. You can pick out individual ideas and mix and match them depending on the needs of your class. The activities include suggestions for how they can be differentiated or used for assessment. **Homework ideas** are also provided.

Starter idea

1 Getting started (5–10 minutes)

Resources: Photo of frog skeleton from Learner's Book.

Description: Show learners the photo of the frog skeleton and ask them to read the accompanying questions.

Use the 'Think-pair-share' method to allow learners to think about their answers for a minute or two, then discuss their answer with a partner before sharing their answers with the class.

Main teaching ideas

1 What is a skeleton? (10 minutes)

Learning intention: Know that the skeleton supports the body; describe how the body would look without a skeleton

Resources: A life-sized paper outline drawing of the human body; a picture of frame buildings, for example traditional homes in Thailand and Japan, a car port or gazebo.

Description: Show the class a life-sized paper outline drawing of the body. Hold up the paper outline and then let it go. Ask learners to describe what their bodies would be like without a skeleton.

The **Language support** feature contains suggestions for how to support learners with English as an additional language. The vocabulary terms and definitions from the Learner's Book are also collected here.

LANGUAGE SUPPORT

You can make a set of flash cards for learners to use to match the new terms learnt in this topic with their meanings.

bones: hard, strong parts inside our body that give our body shape and keep us upright

The **Cross-curricular links** feature provides suggestions for linking to other subject areas.

CROSS-CURRICULAR LINKS

Main teaching ideas 1 and 3 both link with movement and exercise in Physical Education.

> **Digital Classroom:** If you have access to Digital Classroom, these links will suggest when to use the various multimedia enhancements and interactive activities.

Digital resources to download

This Teacher's Resource includes a range of digital materials that you can download from Cambridge GO. (For more information about how to access and use your digital resource, please see inside front cover.) This icon ⬇ indicates material that is available from Cambridge GO.

Helpful documents for planning include:

- **Letter for parents – Introducing the Cambridge Primary resources:** a template letter for parents, introducing the Cambridge Primary Science resources.
- **Lesson plan template:** a Word document that you can use for planning your lessons. Examples of completed lesson plans are also provided.
- **Curriculum framework correlation:** a table showing how the Cambridge Primary Science resources map to the Cambridge Primary Science curriculum framework.
- **Scheme of work:** a suggested scheme of work that you can use to plan teaching throughout the year.

Each unit includes:

- **Differentiated worksheets:** these worksheets are provided in variations that cater for different abilities. Worksheets labelled 'A' are intended to support less confident learners, worksheets labelled 'B' should cater for the majority of learners, while worksheets labelled 'C' are designed to challenge more confident learners. For some worksheets, 'Help' and 'Stretch' sheets are provided in addition to the worksheet activity, which can be given to less confident or more confident learners as appropriate. Answer sheets are provided.
- **Language worksheets:** these worksheets provide language support and can be particularly helpful for learners with English as an additional language. Answers sheets are provided.
- **Resource sheets:** these include templates and any other materials that support activities described in the teaching notes.
- **End-of-unit tests:** these provide quick checks of the learner's understanding of the concepts covered in the unit. Answers are provided. Advice on using these tests formatively is given in the Assessment for Learning section of this Teacher's Resource.

Additionally, the Teacher's Resource includes:

- **Diagnostic check and answers:** a test to use at the beginning of the year to discover the level that learners are working at. The results of this test can inform your planning.
- **Mid-point test and answers:** a test to use after learners have studied half the units in the Learner's Book. You can use this test to check whether there are areas that you need to go over again.
- **End-of-year test and answers:** a test to use after learners have studied all units in the Learner's Book. You can use this test to check whether there are areas that you need to go over again, and to help inform your planning for the next year.
- **Answers to Learner's Book questions**
- **Answers to Workbook questions**
- **Glossary**

In addition, you can find more detailed information about teaching approaches.

📹 **Video** is available through the Digital Classroom.

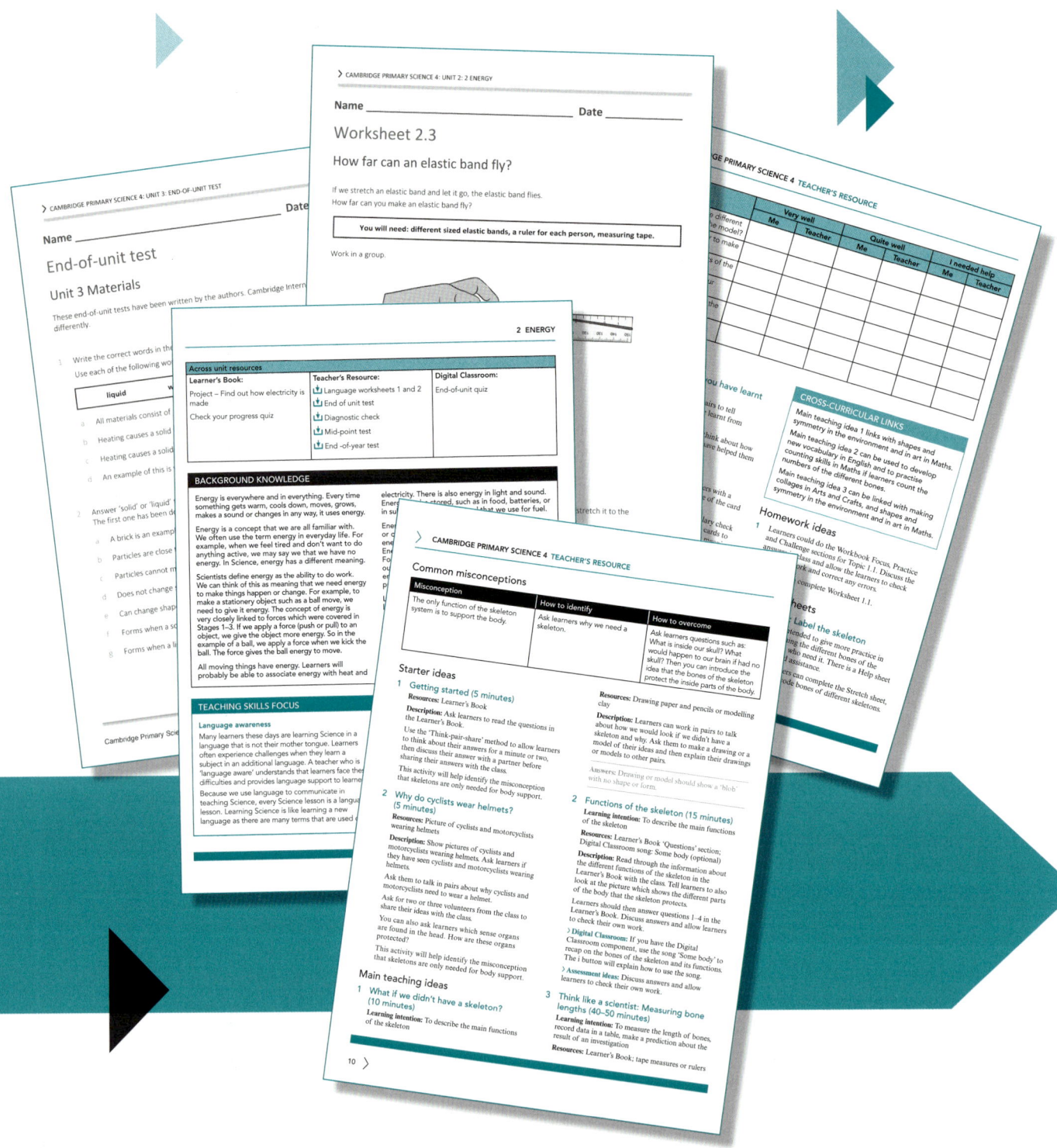

> About the curriculum framework

*The information in this section is based on the Cambridge Primary Science curriculum framework (0097) from 2020. You should always refer to the appropriate curriculum framework document for the year of your learners' examination to confirm the details and for more information. Visit **www.cambridgeinternational.orglprimary** to find out more.*

The Cambridge Primary Science curriculum framework has been updated for teaching from September 2021. The Primary Science curriculum framework has been developed to support learners in building their understanding about the natural world, particularly how to explain and investigate phenomena.

The curriculum framework incorporates three components:

- four content strands (Biology, Chemistry, Physics, and Earth and Space)
- a skills strand called Thinking and Working Scientifically
- a context strand called Science in Context

Biology, Chemistry, Physics and Earth and Space provide the scientific knowledge content, which gradually develops from stage 1 to stage 6 and provides a smooth progression towards Cambridge Lower Secondary study.

The Thinking and Working Scientifically learning objectives focus on the key scientific skills that are developed throughout the course. This strand is split into five types of scientific enquiry:

- observing over time
- identifying and classifying
- pattern seeking
- fair testing, and
- research

Science in Context allows for personal, local and global contexts to be incorporated into scientific study, making science relevant to the contexts that learners are familiar with. This element of the curriculum framework offers great flexibility to teachers and learners around the world.

The Cambridge Primary Science curriculum framework promotes a learner-led, enquiry-based approach. Practical work is a valuable part of science learning and develops learners' investigation skills such as observation, measurement and equipment handling.

> About the assessment

Information about the assessment of the Cambridge Primary Science curriculum framework is available on the Cambridge Assessment International Education website. www.cambridgeinternational.org/primary

› Approaches to learning and teaching

The following are the key pedagogies underpinning our course content and how we understand and define them.

Active learning

Active learning is a pedagogical practice that places student learning at its centre. It focuses on how students learn, not just on what they learn. We, as teachers, need to encourage learners to 'think hard', rather than passively receive information. Active learning encourages learners to take responsibility for their learning and supports them in becoming independent and confident learners in school and beyond.

Assessment for Learning

Assessment for Learning (AfL) is a teaching approach that generates feedback which can be used to improve learners' performance. Learners become more involved in the learning process and, from this, gain confidence in what they are expected to learn and to what standard. We, as teachers, gain insights into a learner's level of understanding of a particular concept or topic, which helps to inform how we support their progression.

Differentiation

Differentiation is usually presented as a teaching practice where teachers think of learners as individuals and learning as a personalised process. Whilst precise definitions can vary, typically the core aim of differentiation is viewed as ensuring that all learners, no matter their ability, interest or context, make progress towards their learning outcomes.

It is about using different approaches and appreciating the differences in learners to help them make progress. Teachers therefore need to be responsive, and willing and able to adapt their teaching to meet the needs of their learners.

Language awareness

For many learners, English is an additional language. It might be their second or perhaps their third language. Depending on the school context, students might be learning all or just some of their subjects through English. For all learners, regardless of whether they are learning through their first language or an additional language, language is a vehicle for learning. It is through language that students access the learning intentions of the lesson and communicate their ideas. It is our responsibility, as teachers, to ensure that language doesn't present a barrier to learning.

Metacognition

Metacognition describes the processes involved when learners plan, monitor, evaluate and make changes to their own learning behaviours. These processes help learners to think about their own learning more explicitly and ensure that they are able to meet a learning goal that they have identified themselves or that we, as teachers, have set.

Skills for Life

How do we prepare learners to succeed in a fast-changing world? To collaborate with people from around the globe? To create innovation as technology increasingly takes over routine work? To use advanced thinking skills in the face of more complex challenges? To show resilience in the face of constant change? At Cambridge, we are responding to educators who have asked for a way to understand how all these different approaches to life skills and competencies relate to their teaching. We have grouped these skills into six main Areas of Competency that can be incorporated into teaching, and have examined the different stages of the learning journey and how these competencies vary across each stage.

These six key areas are:

*   Creativity - finding new ways of doing things, and solutions to problems
*   Collaboration - the ability to work well with others
*   Communication - speaking and presenting confidently and participating effectively in meetings
*   Critical thinking - evaluating what is heard or read, and linking ideas constructively
*   Learning to learn - developing the skills to learn more effectively
*   Social responsibilities - contributing to social groups, and being able to talk to and work with people from other cultures.

Cambridge learner and teacher attributes

This course helps develop the following Cambridge learner and teacher attributes.

Cambridge learners	Cambridge teachers
Confident in working with information and ideas – their own and those of others.	**Confident** in teaching their subject and engaging each student in learning.
Responsible for themselves, responsive to and respectful of others.	**Responsible** for themselves, responsive to and respectful of others.
Reflective as learners, developing their ability to learn.	**Reflective** as learners themselves, developing their practice.
Innovative and equipped for new and future challenges.	**Innovative** and equipped for new and future challenges.
Engaged intellectually and socially, ready to make a difference.	**Engaged** intellectually, professionally and socially, ready to make a difference.

Reproduced from Developing the Cambridge learner attributes *with permission from Cambridge Assessment International Education.*

More information about these approaches to learning and teaching is available to download from Cambridge GO (as part of this Teacher's Resource).

> Setting up for success

Our aim is to support better learning in the classroom with resources that allow for increased learner autonomy while supporting teachers to facilitate student learning.

Through an active learning approach of enquiry-led tasks, open-ended questions and opportunities to externalise thinking in a variety of ways, learners will develop analysis, evaluation and problem-solving skills.

Some ideas to consider to encourage an active learning environment are as follows:

- Set up seating to make group work easy.

- Create classroom routines to help learners to transition between different types of activity efficiently, e.g. move from pair work to listening to the teacher to independent work.

- Source mini-whiteboards, which allow you to get feedback from all learners rapidly.

- Start a portfolio for each learner, keeping key pieces of work to show progress at parent–teacher days.

- Have a display area with learner work and vocab flashcards.

Planning for active learning

We recommend the following approach to planning. A blank Lesson Plan Template is available to download to help with this approach.

1 **Plan learning intentions and success criteria:** these are the most important feature of the lesson. Teachers and learners need to know where they are going in order to plan a route to get there.

2 **Plan language support:** think about strategies to help learners overcome the language demands of the lesson so that language doesn't present a barrier to learning.

3 **Plan starter activities:** include a 'hook' or starter to engage learners using imaginative strategies. This should be an activity where all learners are active from the start of the lesson.

4 **Plan main activities:** during the lesson, try to: give clear instructions, with modelling and written support; coordinate logical and orderly transitions between activities; make sure that learning is active and all learners are engaged ; create opportunities for discussion around key concepts.

5 **Plan assessment for learning and differentiation:** use a wide range of Assessment for Learning techniques and adapt activities to a wide range of abilities. Address misconceptions at appropriate points and give meaningful oral and written feedback which learners can act on.

6 **Plan reflection and plenary:** at the end of each activity and at the end of each lesson, try to: ask learners to reflect on what they have learnt compared to the beginning of the lesson; build on and extend this learning.

7 **Plan homework:** if setting homework, it can be used to consolidate learning from the previous lesson or to prepare for the next lesson

To help planning using this approach, a blank Lesson plan template is available to download from Cambridge GO (as part of this Teacher's Resource). There are also examples of completed lesson plans.

For more guidance on setting up for success and planning, please explore the Professional Development pages of our website **www.cambridge.org/education/PD**

> 1 Living things

Unit plan

Topic	Approximate number of learning hours	Outline of learning content	Resources
1.1 Bones and skeletons	1.5	• Names and positions of some bones in the human skeleton and names and positions of bones	**Learner's Book:** Activity: Finding your bones Think like a scientist: Make a model skeleton **Workbook:** Topic 1.1 ⬇ Worksheet 1.1
1.2 Why we need a skeleton	2	• Functions of the skeleton • Measure length of bones, record data in a table	**Learner's Book:** Think like a scientist: Measuring bone lengths **Workbook:** Topic 1.2 ⬇ Worksheets 1.2A, 1.2B and 1.2C ⬇ Unit 1 wordsearch template **Digital Classroom:** Song – Some body
1.3 Skeletons and movement	2	• How the skeleton and muscles work to cause movement • Importance of exercise for good health	**Learner's Book:** Activity: Find out how muscles work in pairs Think like a scientist: Make a model of arm muscles **Workbook:** Topic 1.3 **Digital Classroom:** Animation – How do our muscles work?
1.4 Different kinds of skeletons	1.5	• Vertebrates and invertebrates	**Learner's Book:** Think like a scientist: Identify vertebrates and invertebrates **Workbook:** Topic 1.4 ⬇ Worksheet 1.4 **Digital Classroom:** Video – Do all animals have bones Animation – Identification keys Video – Animals without bones

Topic	Approximate number of learning hours	Outline of learning content	Resources
1.5 Medicines and infectious diseases	2	• Using medicines safely to treat illnesses • Knowing that plants, animals and humans can get infectious diseases • Knowing that vaccinations can prevent some infectious diseases	**Learner's Book:** Think like a scientist 1: How to take medicines safely Think like a scientist 2: Research information about vaccinations **Workbook:** Topic 1.5 ⬇ Worksheet 1.5 **Digital Classroom:** Science investigators video – How do people take medicines?

Across unit resources		
Learner's Book: Project: Earthworm farming Check your progress quiz	**Teacher's Resource** ⬇ Language worksheet 1 & 2 ⬇ End-of-unit test ⬇ Diagnostic check ⬇ Mid-point test ⬇ End-of-year test	**Digital Classroom:** End-of-unit quiz

BACKGROUND KNOWLEDGE

The skeleton is the structure inside our body that is made up of bones. The main functions of the skeleton are to provide a frame that supports the body; to protect internal organs such as the heart, lungs and brain; and to allow movement. The bones of the skeleton also grow, which allows us to grow.

Humans and animals that have a backbone or spine are known as vertebrates. The name 'vertebrates' comes from the scientific word for the bones of the spine, which are called vertebrae. Animals that do not have a backbone are called invertebrates.

Some invertebrates have exoskeletons. Exoskeletons are hard outside, or external, skeletons that cover the bodies of invertebrates such as insects, spiders, millipedes, crabs and crayfish. Other invertebrates have soft bodies with no exoskeleton, for example worms, jellyfish and slugs.

Muscles make the body move. Muscles joined to the bones of the skeleton work in pairs to allow the bone to move. Muscles cause movement when they get shorter (contract) and pull on the bone they are

joined to. When one muscle in a pair contracts, the other muscles relaxes and becomes longer.

Other muscles, such as the heart, are not involved in movement.

Muscles cannot push; they only pull on bones to allow movement. This is why muscles act in pairs. One muscle pulls the bone in one direction and another muscle pulls it in the opposite direction.

Body movement is important for keeping our heart and lungs healthy. It has other benefits too, such as improving the strength of muscles and bones, increasing body flexibility and helping to prevent disease such as diabetes and heart disease. Many young people today spend a lot of time sitting still while watching TV or playing games on their phones or computers. They also spend several hours each day sitting in class. Body movement improves our feeling of well-being and allows the mind to focus and concentrate better. Try to create opportunities in your class for learners to active whenever possible.

CONTINUED

It is very important to use medicines safely and correctly. Always follow the instructions given for taking the medicine. Do not use prescribed medicine that is meant for someone else. Also do not use out-of-date medicines. Be sure to store medicines in a place where children cannot reach them.

Medicines are used to treat or prevent diseases. Infectious diseases are caused by tiny micro-organisms that we commonly call germs. The germs enter the body and affect the way the body works, making us ill. For example, the germs that cause flu affect our nose, throat and lungs. Plants, animals and people can all get infectious diseases.

TEACHING SKILLS FOCUS

Active learning

Active learning is a form of learning in which learners become more directly involved in the learning process. Younger learners, in particular, find it difficult to listen and concentrate for more than about five minutes at a time if they are not actively doing something.

These are some strategies for active learning you can use in your lessons, particularly at the start and end of a lesson:

- Have a prior knowledge 'Round Robin' at the start of new topic or lesson. Learners pass around a piece of paper on which they write down anything they already know about the topic.

- Spend a few minutes on a 'Think-pair-share' exercise in which you ask a question, for example, 'Why do we need skeleton?' Learners think about their own answer, discuss it with a classmate and finally share it with the class as part of a formal discussion. This strategy can be used at the start or the end of a lesson. This strategy will also work well for the 'Getting started' feature at the start of each topic in the Learner's Book.

- Pause briefly during an explanation to ask learners questions about the lesson. This strategy is used in the Digital Classroom investigation videos and animations, where learners are given the opportunity to think about the answer to a question while the video is paused.

- Do a quick check at the end of a lesson. Let learners stand and quickly say one thing they have learnt in the lesson before sitting down.

- Make a set of 'exit' tickets that learners can pick up at the end of a lesson. They have to hand you back a 'ticket' with an answer to a question. Some examples are:

  - Today I learnt…

  - I would have liked…

  - Now I understand…

Learners at this level love to learn about themselves and their bodies, which provides opportunities for active learning in this unit. For example, you can use the active learning strategy of peer-to-peer learning to get learners to demonstrate and explain to one another, or to the class, what they found out when they explored the bones of their skeletons and how their muscles work. Peer learning is discussed further in the notes for Unit 2.

Any hands-on task can be used for active learning, although just doing the task or activity does not necessarily mean that learning has taken place. Practical work and other hands-on activities need to be followed up by discussion and questioning. Getting learners to make predictions before they start an investigation is another way of involving them in the learning process.

1.1 Bones and skeletons

LEARNING PLAN

Learning objectives	Learning intentions	Success criteria
4Bs.01 Identify some of the important bones in the human body (limited to skull, jaw, rib cage, hip, spine, leg bones and arm bones).	• To be able to name some of the bones in our body. • To be able to point out where some of the main bones are found in our body.	• Learners can identify the skull, jaw, spine, rib cage, hip, arm bones and leg bones.
4TWSm.01 Know that models are not fully representative of a real-world situation and/or scientific idea.	• To make a model skeleton. • To be able to think about how a model is different to the real thing.	• Learners can make a model of a skeleton. • Learners can explain how a model is different to the real thing.

LANGUAGE SUPPORT

There are many new terms in this topic. You will find these listed below, in the Learner's Book and explained in the glossary. Make sure you are familiar with the terms before you teach the topic.

You can make a set of flash cards for learners to use to match the new terms learnt in this topic with their meanings. Write the word on one side of the card and its meaning on the other side. Get learners to test one another.

- **bones** – hard, strong parts inside our body that give our body shape and keep us upright
- **frame** – something that gives support and shape from the inside
- **hip** – the bone that joins the leg to the upper part of the body
- **jaw** – the skull bone that moves when we eat or talk
- **model** – an object or drawing that helps us understand how something works or see what something looks like that we can't see in real life
- **rib cage** – the bones of the chest
- **skeleton** – the bones inside our body that are joined together to form a frame
- **skull** – the bones of the head
- **spine** – the bones of the back

Common misconceptions

Misconception	How to identify	How to overcome
Bones are not living.	Ask learners to describe bones. Are they living or non-living?	Ask learners if their bones are the same size now as when they were babies. The answer is no, which shows that bones grow. Learners should recall from S3 that growth is a life process.

Starter ideas

1   Getting started (5–10 minutes)

Resources: Photo of frog skeleton from Learner's Book.

Description: Show learners the photo of the frog skeleton and ask them to read the accompanying questions.

Use the 'Think-pair-share' method to allow learners to think about their answers for a minute or two, then discuss their answer with a partner before sharing their answers with the class.

2   Know your bones (5 minutes)

Resources: Paper outline of human body.

Description: Give each learner a paper outline of the human body. Ask learners to draw the different bones in their body that they know of on the outline.

Main teaching ideas

1   What is a skeleton? (10 minutes)

Learning intention: Know that the skeleton supports the body; describe how the body would look without a skeleton

Resources: A life-sized paper outline drawing of the human body; a picture of frame buildings, for example traditional homes in Thailand and Japan, a car port or gazebo.

Description: Show the class a life-sized paper outline drawing of the body. Hold up the paper outline and then let it go. Ask learners to describe what their bodies would be like without a skeleton.

Ask learners to think about buildings that they have seen being built covered in scaffolding or buildings that have frames for support, such as traditional homes in Thailand and Japan. Point out that rest of the house is built around the frame. Explain that our skeleton works in the same way to support our bodies.

> **Practical guidance:** You can make a paper outline of the body by asking a learner to lie on a piece of paper and draw round the outline of the learner. Be aware of cultural sensitivities when doing this though.

Answers: Our bodies would be soft and floppy and could not stay upright, like the paper outline.

---

2   Activity: Finding your bones (15–20 minutes)

Learning intention: Identify and name the skull, jaw, rib cage, hip, spine, leg bones, arm bones

Resources: Picture of skeleton from Learner's Book; life-size model skeleton (optional)

Description: Tell learners they are going to feel the bones in their own skeletons.

Point to the different bones in the picture of the skeleton in the Learner's Book so that learners know where to find those bones in their own bodies.

Be sensitive to learners who are overweight and may have difficulty in feeling their ribs. They will be able to feel the rib bones with their fingers, but not as easily as other learners. It might be easiest for them to feel the ribs by stretching up one arm and then using the opposite hand to feel the ribs on the stretched side. Demonstrate this action and suggest that the whole class feel their ribs in this way. Tell them to push firmly on their skin until they feel the rib bones.

Learners will not be able to feel all their ribs and vertebrae, but they should get the idea that there are many of each of these bones. The skull should feel like a single bone but explain that it is made of several bones fused together.

Learners will be able to feel two bones in the lower arm and one bone in the upper arm.

The upper leg bone (thigh bone) is longer and bigger than the lower leg bones.

Learners should point out and name the skull, jaw, rib cage, spine, arm bones and leg bones.

Once learners have completed the activity, discuss the observation that the skeleton is made of many bones of different shapes and sizes. Discuss the reason for this after learners have completed question 3 in the 'Questions' section in the Learner's Book.

> **Practical guidance:** If possible, borrow a life-size model skeleton from a local secondary school or doctors' surgery.

Show the skeleton to the class. Point out the skull, rib cage, spine, hip bones and arm and leg bones. Then ask learners to try to count the number of bones in the spine, the rib cage and the skull. You can also ask them to look at the sizes and shapes of the different bones.

> **Differentiation ideas:** All learners should be able to find and name the bones in their body. You can support any learners who are struggling by allowing them to work in pairs with more confident learners to find and name the bones of their skeleton.

Use the 'Questions' section for differentiation purposes. All learners should be able to answer questions 1 and 2. Less confident learners may not be able to answer question 3 without assistance. More advanced learners should be able to question 4.

> **Assessment ideas:** You could use the '1-2-3 Fingers' strategy to find out if learners can identify and name the skull, jaw, rib cage, hip, spine, leg bones and arm bones. Get learners to hold up fingers to respond:

1 finger = I can't do it

2 fingers = I can do some of it

3 fingers = I can do it all

If a show of fingers is not culturally unacceptable, you could use small red (I can't do it), yellow (I can do some of it) and green (I can do it all) cards instead.

You can use Exercises 1–3 of Workbook 1.1 Bones and skeletons to assess learners'
level of understanding of the main bones in the body.

3 Think like a scientist: Make a model skeleton (30 minutes)

Learning intention: To follow instructions to make a model skeleton; say why a model is both the same as and different to the real object

Resources: Learner's Book 1.1 Bones and skeletons; examples of models, e.g. a model car or a globe of the Earth; plastic drinking straws and bottle tops, modelling clay or different shapes of pasta; scissors, black construction paper or stiff card, paper glue, white paper, a pen

Description: Show examples of models to the learners. Ask the learners what real-life things the models represent. Ask how the models are the same as the real thing. How are they different to the real thing?

Show learners the picture of the skeleton in the Learner's Book. Tell them to take note of the position, size and shape of the different bones in the skeleton. Tell learners that they should cut the straws into different lengths to make 'bones' for their skeletons. Ask them how they think they will use the bottle tops (for the skull). If learners are using pasta shapes, tell them to look for pasta shapes that are similar shapes to the different bones.

Learners should arrange the lengths of plastic straws and bottle tops or pasta shapes to make the form of a human skeleton. It does not need to be accurate but should show the general body form with a skull, jaw, spine, ribs, arms, legs and hips.

Learners should then answer the questions in the 'Questions' section.

> **Practical guidance:** This is a learner-led activity. Learners should work in groups of 4–5.

> **Differentiation ideas:** You can support less confident learners by placing them in mixed-ability groups. Encourage group members to work co-operatively to make the model so that all learners have a role to play.

> **Assessment ideas:** You can use the assessment checklist given here for both self-assessment and teacher assessment.

How well did I:	Very well		Quite well		I needed help	
	Me	Teacher	Me	Teacher	Me	Teacher
plan how to use the different materials to make the model?						
work with my partner to make the model?						
label the different parts of the model?						
think of ways to make our model better?						
explain how the model is the same as a real skeleton?						
explain how the model is different to a real skeleton?						

Plenary ideas

1 Tell your partner what you have learnt (5 minutes)

Description: Learners work in pairs to tell each other three things they have learnt from the topic.

> **Reflection ideas:** Ask learners to think about how the different activities in the topic have helped them learn about skeletons and models.

2 Flash cards (5 minutes)

Resources: Sets of flash cards for learners with a new term learnt in this topic on one side of the card and the meanings on the other side.

Description: Use this activity as a vocabulary check for learners. Learners should use the flash cards to test one another. They should read out the meaning of a term to partner who must say the term. Learners in the pair can take turns in reading and naming the term. If you only have one set of cards, you can use them for a whole class plenary activity in which you read out the meanings of the terms and ask learners to say the term. Or you can say the term and get learners to explain the meaning of the term.

> **Assessment ideas:** Learners can note how many of the new words they know. They can look up the words they didn't know in the glossary.

CROSS-CURRICULAR LINKS

Main teaching idea 1 links with shapes and symmetry in the environment and in art in Maths.

Main teaching idea 2 can be used to develop new vocabulary in English and to practise counting skills in Maths if learners count the numbers of the different bones.

Main teaching idea 3 can be linked with making collages in Arts and Crafts, and shapes and symmetry in the environment and in art in Maths.

Homework ideas

1   Learners could do the Workbook Focus, Practice and Challenge sections for Topic 1.1. Discuss the answers in class and allow the learners to check their own work and correct any errors.

2   Learners can complete Worksheet 1.1.

Topic worksheets

Worksheet 1.1: Label the skeleton

This worksheet is intended to give more practice in identifying and naming the different bones of the skeleton for learners who need it. There is a Help sheet for learners who need assistance.

More confident learners can complete the Stretch sheet, in which they colour code bones of different skeletons.

1.2 Why we need a skeleton

LEARNING PLAN

Learning objectives	Learning intention	Success criteria
4Bs.03 Describe some of the important functions of skeletons (limited to protecting and supporting organs, enabling movement and giving shape to the body).	• To be able to describe the main functions of the skeleton.	• Learners can describe the main functions of the skeleton as protecting organs, allowing movement, giving shape to the body and supporting organs during activity. • Learners can understand that we grow because our skeleton grows.
4TWSc.05 Take measurements in standard units, describing the advantage of standard units over non-standard units.	• To be able to measure the length of bones. To say why using standard units is better.	• Learners can measure the length of bones. Learners can say why it is better to measure in standard units
4TWSc.08 Collect and record observations and/or measurements in tables and diagrams.	• To be able to record data in a table.	• Learners can record data in a table.
4TWSp.03 Make a prediction describing some possible outcomes of an enquiry.	• To be able to make a prediction about the result of an investigation.	• Learners can make a prediction about the result of an investigation.

LANGUAGE SUPPORT

Learners will use the following words in the topic:
- **function** – the job or use of something, for example the function of a pen is to write
- **length** – how long something is; for example, the length of a ruler is 30 cm
- **muscles** – parts of the body that are joined to bones and allow us to move
- **organs** – parts inside the body that do different jobs

- **protect** – keep safe from harm, for example, a jacket will protect you from the cold
- **support** – to hold up something so that it doesn't fall down

Most of the words listed above are used in everyday speech or writing. Give learners the opportunity to use these words correctly by asking them to write or complete sentences using the words.

Common misconceptions

Misconception	How to identify	How to overcome
The only function of the skeleton system is to support the body.	Ask learners why we need a skeleton.	Ask learners questions such as: What is inside our skull? What would happen to our brain if had no skull? Then you can introduce the idea that the bones of the skeleton protect the inside parts of the body.

Starter ideas

1 Getting started (5 minutes)

Resources: Learner's Book

Description: Ask learners to read the questions in the Learner's Book.

Use the 'Think-pair-share' method to allow learners to think about their answers for a minute or two, then discuss their answer with a partner before sharing their answers with the class.

This activity will help identify the misconception that skeletons are only needed for body support.

2 Why do cyclists wear helmets? (5 minutes)

Resources: Picture of cyclists and motorcyclists wearing helmets

Description: Show pictures of cyclists and motorcyclists wearing helmets. Ask learners if they have seen cyclists and motorcyclists wearing helmets.

Ask them to talk in pairs about why cyclists and motorcyclists need to wear a helmet.

Ask for two or three volunteers from the class to share their ideas with the class.

You can also ask learners which sense organs are found in the head. How are these organs protected?

This activity will help identify the misconception that skeletons are only needed for body support.

Main teaching ideas

1 What if we didn't have a skeleton? (10 minutes)

Learning intention: To describe the main functions of the skeleton

Resources: Drawing paper and pencils or modelling clay

Description: Learners can work in pairs to talk about how we would look if we didn't have a skeleton and why. Ask them to make a drawing or a model of their ideas and then explain their drawings or models to other pairs.

Answers: Drawing or model should show a 'blob' with no shape or form.

2 Functions of the skeleton (15 minutes)

Learning intention: To describe the main functions of the skeleton

Resources: Learner's Book 'Questions' section; Digital Classroom song: Some body (optional)

Description: Read through the information about the different functions of the skeleton in the Learner's Book with the class. Tell learners to also look at the picture which shows the different parts of the body that the skeleton protects.

Learners should then answer questions 1–4 in the Learner's Book. Discuss answers and allow learners to check their own work.

> **Digital Classroom:** If you have the Digital Classroom component, use the song 'Some body' to recap on the bones of the skeleton and its functions. The i button will explain how to use the song.

> **Assessment ideas:** Discuss answers and allow learners to check their own work.

3 Think like a scientist: Measuring bone lengths (40–50 minutes)

Learning intention: To measure the length of bones, record data in a table, make a prediction about the result of an investigation

Resources: Learner's Book; tape measures or rulers

Description: In this activity learners will measure the length of arm bones.

Get learners to read the instructions for the activity before they begin. Tell them to ask you to explain any steps that are not clear to them. Learners then copy the table, do the measuring and record their results in the table, and answer the questions on the Learner's Book.

Also discuss with learners the units they should use to measure the bones. They will be familiar with the use of non-standard and standard units from Stage 3. Remind them that in the past people used parts of the human body such as hands, arms, fingers and legs as the units of measurement for length. For example, a cubit was the length of the arm from the elbow to the tip of the middle finger. We now measure length in units such as mm, cm or metres. Because arm and hand lengths vary, non-standard measurements like the cubit are not very accurate.

Using standard measurements makes measuring more accurate, which is important to scientists. Using non-standard measurements can also cause confusion if other people are not using the same units for measuring or do not understand the units you are using. Using standard measurements also allows us to compare our data with other people's.

You could also introduce the pattern seeking method of scientific enquiry in this activity by asking learners if boys' bones are longer than girls' bones. Learners should compare the measurements for boys and girls and see if they find a pattern.

> **Practical guidance:** Learners should work in pairs or groups of four (they will need a partner to measure). Each pair or group will need a tape measure.

Demonstrate how to use the tape measure by measuring the length of one of the learners' upper arm bones.

Remember that the measurements will not be completely accurate as you will not be able to measure to the very ends of some of the bones. The easiest bone to measure is the outer bone of the lower arm (ulna). The bone starts in the wrist (you can see and feel the rounded end of the bone) and ends in the elbow.

It is best for learners to measure the bone lengths of learners of their own gender within the group. This will avoid overstepping any cultural or religious boundaries regarding contact between males and females.

If you do not have enough tape measures, learners can use 30 cm rulers to measure the length of the bones.

> **Differentiation ideas:** Higher-achieving learners can draw a bar chart or bar chart of their results, or

measure other bones, such as the circumference of the skull to extend their table.

> **Assessment ideas:** Learners can answer the 'How am I doing?' questions in the Learner's Book to find out if they have achieved the learning intentions for the activity.

Plenary ideas

1 What have I learnt today? (5 minutes)

Description: Ask learners to tell you one new thing that they have learnt in the lesson today. (If the class is large, there will not be time to ask everyone, so use hands-up or choose a few learners individually.)

2 Wordsearch (5 minutes)

Resources: Unit 1 wordsearch template

Description: Make a copy of the Unit 1 wordsearch template for each learner. The wordsearch contains key words learnt in the topic. Learners should use the clues to find the words.

Clues

1 body parts that let us move (muscles)

2 the job of something (function)

3 how long something is (length)

4 the skull does this for the brain (protects)

5 the brain and heart are examples of these kinds of body parts (organs)

6 the job of the skeleton is to hold up the rest of the body (support)

Answers

W	M	T	Y	U	O	P	S
F	U	N	C	T	I	O	N
P	S	D	F	G	H	H	K
R	C	L	X	H	A	V	N
O	L	E	N	G	T	H	F
T	E	C	V	N	M	O	L
E	S	U	P	P	O	R	T
C	Q	W	E	G	H	G	I
T	U	D	J	K	L	A	C
S	S	D	R	I	P	N	V
B	N	M	Y	E	S	S	T

> **Assessment ideas:** Let learners check their own answers and make any corrections needed.

> **Reflection ideas:** Ask learners: Was it easy to find the words in the wordsearch? Were there any words you did not know the meaning of? Were there any words you did not know how to spell?

Homework ideas

1 Learners could complete the Workbook Focus, Practice and Challenge sections for Topic 1.2. In the next lesson, discuss answers. Allow learners to swap answers and check one another's work.

2 Learners can complete Worksheet 1.2A, B or C, depending on their confidence. Provide answer sheets for learners to check their own work.

Topic worksheets

Worksheet 1.2A: Draw a graph of bone length

This worksheet gives support to less confident learners as the data table and graph framework are complete and a sample bar has been drawn.

Worksheet 1.2B: Draw a graph of bone length

This worksheet is suitable for learners who are confident at drawing and reading bar graphs.

Worksheet 1.2C: Draw a graph of bone length

Higher-achieving learners can do this worksheet. They will have to fill in the results table themselves, draw the graph and answer questions.

1.3 Skeletons and movement

LEARNING PLAN

Learning objectives	Learning intention	Success criteria
4Bs.02 Know that bones move because pairs of muscles that are attached to them contract and relax.	• To be able to explain how muscles work to make us move. • To be able to observe how muscles change when we move.	• Learners can understand that muscles work in pairs. • Learners can explain how muscles work by pulling on bones. • Learners can understand that when one muscle in a pair contracts, the other muscle in the pair relaxes. • Learners can observe that muscles get shorter and fatter when they contract. • Learners can observe that muscles get longer and thinner when they relax.

CONTINUED

Learning objectives	Learning intention	Success criteria
4Bp.04 Describe the importance of movement in maintaining human health.	• To be able to find out that movement is good for our health	• Learners can say how movement keeps us healthy.
4TWSm.01 Know models are not fully representative of a real work situation and/or scientific idea.	• To be able to explain how a model of muscle action is similar and different to real life muscle action.	• Learners can make and use a model to demonstrate muscle action. • Learners can explain how the model is similar and different to real muscle action.
4TWSm.02 Use models to show relationships quantities or scale.	• To be able to use a model to show how muscles and bones work together to allow us to move.	• Learners can use a model to show how muscles and bones work together to allow us to move.

LANGUAGE SUPPORT

The two important main new words in the topic are:

• **contract** – when muscles get shorter and fatter. Muscles feel hard when they contract.

• **relax** – when muscles get longer and thinner. Muscles feel soft when they relax.

Be sure to get learners to use the words 'contract' and 'relax' when they describe and explain muscle action.

Common misconceptions

Misconception	How to identify	How to overcome
Muscles work by pulling and pushing.	Ask learners to demonstrate how the 'muscles' work on their model. Ask if the 'muscles' push or pull on the bone.	Complete the Activity 'Find out how muscles work in pairs' and peer assess to correct any incorrect explanations about muscle actions.

Starter ideas

1 Getting started (5 minutes)

Resources: Learner's Book

Description: Read through the Learner's Book with the learners and ask them the questions.

Learners should work in pairs to answer the questions. You can ask learners to put up their hands to volunteer to share their answers.

2 Get moving (5–10 minutes)

Description: Ask learners to show each other a range of movements they can make. Ask them to walk, run on the spot, jump up and down, smile, pick up a pencil and clap hands. If your classroom space is limited, take them outside or into the school hall. Ask learners which parts of the body they use in order to do the different movements. Some learners might suggest muscles, which shows that they have linked the action of muscles with body movement.

Main teaching ideas

1 Feel your muscles work (5 minutes)

Learning intention: To observe and demonstrate how a muscle changes when it contracts and relaxes

Description: Ask learners to wave to a friend, or do a similar action. Tell them that when any part of our body moves, muscles are working.

Explain that muscles work by contracting and relaxing. Get learners to move different parts of their body and feel how the muscles change. Which muscles are hard (contracted) and which are soft (relaxed)?

Answers: There are no correct or incorrect answers. Learners should be able to observe and describe how a muscle changes when it is contracted and relaxed.

---

2 Activity: Find out how muscles work in pairs (20 minutes)

Learning intention: To explain how muscles work in pairs to cause movement; observe and demonstrate how a muscle changes when it contracts and relaxes

Resources: Picture in Learner's Book; Digital Classroom animation: How do our muscles work (optional); a weight, such as a large book (for each group)

Description: Ask learners to look at the pictures of muscle action in the Learner's Book. Get them to try the actions themselves. Ask learners to try and feel the two muscles shown in the pictures on their own arms. It is not necessary for you to name the muscles in the upper arm, but if you feel that learners will be interested and will find knowing the names useful, then do so. The muscle at the front of the upper arm is the biceps muscle. The muscle at the back or underside of the arm is the triceps muscle.

Tell the class that muscles act in pairs and cause movement when they pull on bones. Emphasise the point that muscles cannot push. Then let learners do the activity.

> **Digital Classroom:** If you have access to the Digital Classroom component, use the animation 'How do our muscles work?' to aid learners' understanding of how muscles work together in pairs to allow us to move. The i button will explain how to use the animation.

Once learners have completed the practical part of the activity they can consolidate their understanding of muscle action by answering questions 1–3 in the Learner's Book. For question 2 in which they suggest a fair test, they will have to decide which equipment to use and what to measure. Remind them that that only one factor must be changed and everything else must be kept the same.

> **Practical guidance:** Learners should work in pairs.

Learners should hold their arms quite firmly in order to feel the change in the muscles. Contraction and relaxation of the muscles are more easily observed in well-developed muscles.

Learners should observe that as they lift the weight, the muscle in the front of the upper arm gets fatter and bulges, showing that it is getting shorter. It also feels harder. The muscle at the back of the arm feels softer, and does not bulge. When learners straighten their arms, the muscle at the back of the arm feels harder and gets shorter; the muscle in the front of the upper arm gets longer and feel softer.

> **Differentiation ideas:** More confident learners should be able to answer question 4.

> **Assessment ideas:** Tell learners to ask themselves these questions for them to check if they planned a fair test in question 2:

- Did I change only one thing?
- What thing did I change?
- What things did I keep the same?
- What did I measure?

3 Think like a Scientist: Make a model of arm muscles (40–50 minutes)

Learning intention: Make a model to demonstrate muscle action; explain how the model is different to real arm muscles

Resources: Learner's Book; a piece of thick card, two elastic bands (one longer than the other), a ruler, scissors, a paper fastener (split pin); a stapler and staples, a piece of sticky tack or modelling clay

Description: Tell learners to follow the instructions in the Learner's Book to make a model of their arm to show how two muscles of the upper arm work as a pair when the arm moves at the elbow. The model can demonstrate to learners why, if muscles can only pull, and not push, two muscles are needed to move a bone.

Ask learners to think about how their model is both the same and different to the way the muscles in their own arms work – they should use their models to explain to one another how muscles work to produce movement. Then ask learners to demonstrate end explain their models to you.

Assessment criteria Were you able to:	Yes		Needed help		No	
	Partner	Teacher	Partner	Teacher	Partner	Teacher
identify the parts of the model that represent the muscles?						
describe what happens to the other muscle when one of the elastic muscles contracts?						
explain how the model arm bone lifts?						
explain how the model is different to the way your arm muscles work?						
explain how the model is the same as the way your arm muscles work?						

> **Practical guidance:** Learners should work in pairs.

It is important that the paper fastener is inserted at least 5 cm from the ends of the lengths of cardboard. Learners need to be careful with the sharp point of the split pin. This allows the antagonistic (opposite) action of the elastic band 'muscles' to be clearly demonstrated.

If the elastic bands are pulled too tight, learners will not be able to demonstrate muscle action as their elastic band 'muscles' will be fixed in a contracted position.

> **Differentiation ideas:** Group learners in mixed ability groups so that less confident learners can be encouraged and helped by more confident learners.

> **Assessment ideas:** Learners can work in pairs and use the checklist in the table above to assess one another's explanations. You can also use the checklist to assess learners' work.

Plenary ideas

1 Explain muscle action (5 minutes)

Description: Let learners work in pairs to demonstrate and explain to one another how their muscles work to let them move.

> **Reflection ideas:** Ask learners: How did showing a partner how muscles work to allow us to move help you understand muscle action better?

2 True or false? (5 minutes)

Resources: A set of statements, written or projected on the board

Description: Display a set of statements on the board. Get learners to write true or false or each statement.

Possible statements are:

Your leg can move because there are muscles joined to the leg bones (true).

Muscles help us move because they push and pull on bones (false).

Muscles work in pairs (true).

Muscles get shorter when they contract (true).

Muscles cause movement when they relax (false).

Discuss why each answer is true or false.

> **Assessment ideas:** Let learners check their own answers and correct any errors.

> **Reflection ideas:** You can ask learners to think about these questions:

Think about how you worked in this lesson.

- What did you do that you are proud of?
- What did you find difficult? How did you deal with it?

CROSS-CURRICULAR LINKS

Main teaching ideas 1 and 3 both link with movement and exercise in Physical Education.

Homework ideas

1 Learners could do the Workbook Focus, Practice and Challenge sections for Topic 1.3. In the next lesson, provide learners with answer sheets. Allow learners to check their own answers and make any corrections needed.

2 Learners can make a collage or pictures of activities that they like to do that involve movement. Learners can display their collages or pictures in the classroom and say why they like doing these activities.

3 Learners can answer the questions on 'Movement keeps us healthy' in the Learner's Book. Discuss the answers in class and encourage learners to suggest ways to increase the amount of movement in their daily lives.

1.4 Different kinds of skeletons

LEARNING PLAN

Learning objectives	Learning intention	Success criteria
4Bs.05 Identify vertebrates as animals with a backbone and invertebrates as animals without a backbone.	• To find out the difference between vertebrates and invertebrates.	• Learners can identify vertebrates as animals with a backbone. • Learners can identify invertebrates as animals without a backbone.
4Bs.04 Know that some animals have an exoskeleton.	• To learn about different kinds of skeletons.	• Learners can identify animals that have an exoskeleton.
4TWSc.02 Use keys to identify objects, materials and living things.	• To learn how to use an identification key.	• Learners can use an identification key.
4TWSc.01 Use observations and tests to sort, group and classify objects.	• To be able to use observations to group animals with and without an exoskeleton.	• Learners can group animals with and without an exoskeleton.
4TWSp.02 Know that there are five main types of scientific enquiry (research, fair testing, observing over time, **identifying and classifying**, and pattern seeking).	• To be able to understand how using a key helps scientists to sort living things into groups.	• Learners can say how using a key helps scientists to sort living things into groups.

LANGUAGE SUPPORT

Learners will use the following words in the topic:

- **exoskeleton** – the hard skins or shells on the outside of the bodies of some invertebrates
- **identification key** – a set of questions that allows us to name or group things
- **invertebrate** – an animal that has no backbone or spine
- **vertebrate** – an animal that has a backbone or spine

You can help learners to grasp the meanings of some of the words by linking them with the words they may know. For example, 'exo' means outside. You could talk about the exterior or outside of a building. So an exoskeleton is a skeleton on the outside of the body.

You could also explain that the backbone is made of bones called vertebrae. This is why an animal that has a backbone is called a vertebrate.

Common misconceptions

Misconception	How to identify	How to overcome
Animals with a shell are invertebrates.	Show pictures of a snail, crab and tortoise. Ask if the animals are vertebrates or invertebrates and why.	Show pictures of a tortoise skeleton to show it is a vertebrate even though it has a shell.
Animals without legs/limbs are invertebrates.	Show pictures of a worm, snake and centipede. Ask if the animals are vertebrates or invertebrates and why.	Show pictures of a snake skeleton to show it is a vertebrate even though it has no legs.

Starter ideas

1 Getting started (5 minutes)

Resources: Learner's Book

Description: Read through the Getting started activity in the Learner's Book and ask learners the questions.

Use the 'Think-pair-share' method to allow learners to think about their answers for a minute or two, then discuss their answer with a partner before sharing their answers with the class.

2 Sort the animals (5–10 minutes)

Resources: Digital Classroom video: Do all animals have bones? (optional) Otherwise use pictures of a variety of different animals. The pictures should be of both vertebrates (e.g. fish, cow, cat, chicken, snake) and invertebrates (e.g. earthworm, locust, crab, bee). Aim for eight–ten pictures per group.

> **Digital Classroom:** If you have access to the Digital Classroom component, use the video 'Do all animals have bones?' to practise sorting and grouping animals based on observable features. The i button will explain how to use the video.

Otherwise, show the pictures of the different animals. Ask learners to work in small groups to sort the animals into two different groups. Ask how they decided which group to put each animal in. Ask for a spokesperson for each group to share how they grouped their animals. Use this opportunity to remind learners (from Stages 1 3) about the idea of using identifying features, such as having legs, as a way to sort or group living things.

There are no right or wrong answers, this is just an opportunity to practise sorting and grouping.

Main teaching ideas

1 Vertebrates and invertebrates (15 minutes)

Learning intention: Identify vertebrates as animals with a backbone and invertebrates as animals without a backbone

Resources: Learner's Book

Description: Ask learners if they can name any animals that have bones. Draw on prior knowledge of animals with bones that learners may have eaten, such as chicken, goat or fish.

Introduce the term vertebrates and explain what it means and why we use the term.

Introduce the term invertebrates and explain what it means and why we use the term.

Then ask learners if they can name any animals that are invertebrates. They may give some answers that are not correct. Probe learners' answers by asking why they think the animals they have named have no bones (see section on misconceptions). You may get answers such 'their bodies are soft', which is scientifically acceptable at this level, but look out for unscientific answers such as 'it moves slowly', or 'it has a long body'.

Ask learners to answer questions 1–5 in the Learner's Book.

> **Differentiation ideas:** All learners should be able to answer questions 1–4.

More confident learners should be able to answer question 5.

> **Assessment ideas:** Discuss answers in class. Learners can swap work with a partner and check each other's answers.

2 Sort and group invertebrates (10–15 minutes)

Learning intention: To learn about different kinds of skeletons; identify animals with an exoskeleton; group animals with and without an exoskeleton.

Resources Digital Classroom video: Animals without bones (optional) or pictures of different invertebrates, including some with an exoskeleton and others with no exoskeleton

> **Digital Classroom:** If you have access to the Digital Classroom component, use the video 'Animals without bones' to sort invertebrates into those with exoskeletons and those without exoskeletons. The i button will explain how to use the video.

Otherwise, show the pictures you have found and ask learners to sort and group the animals. Ask:

- How are the animals the same?
- How are they different?
- Ask learners which animals have an exoskeleton. Which animals have no exoskeleton?

As a challenge or extension, ask how the invertebrate animals without an exoskeleton support their bodies. Let learners come up with some ideas. Then explain that these animals have fluid in their bodies that supports them. You can demonstrate this by filling a plastic bag with water. Seal the bag or hold it closed. Ask learners to push on the bag. Can they squash it? Explain that this is how the bodies of invertebrate animals with no exoskeleton are supported. Make it clear to learners that this knowledge is not required for Stage 4.

Answers: Animals with an exoskeleton: for example, beetle, centipede, crab, locust.

Animals with no exoskeleton: for example, earthworm, slug, jellyfish, sea anemone.

> **Assessment ideas:** Ask learners to tell a partner what an exoskeleton is and to name two animals that have an exoskeleton.

3 Think like a scientist: Identify vertebrates and invertebrates (15–20 minutes)

Learning intention: To use an identification key to identify vertebrates and invertebrates

Resources: Pictures and key from Learner's Book; Worksheet 1.4 (optional); Digital Classroom animation: Identification keys (optional)

> **Digital Classroom:** If you have access to the Digital Classroom component, use the animation 'Identification keys' to explain how to use an

identification key to name and identify living things. The i button will explain how to use the animation.

In this activity, learners will be using the identifying and classifying type of scientific enquiry.

Work step by step through the example key in the Learner's Book. Explain each step to learners.

Let learners work in pairs to identify vertebrates and invertebrates in the activity key. They can then answer questions 1–3 in the Learner's Book.

Scientists can sort them into groups by looking at the features that they share.

Learners could complete Worksheet 1.4 once they've finished the investigation. There is a Help sheet for less confident learners and more confident learners can be challenged to answer the question on the Stretch sheet.

⟩ **Differentiation ideas:** All learners should be able to answer questions 1 and 2.

More confident learners should be able to answer question 3.

⟩ **Assessment ideas:** Learners can use the 'How am I doing?' feature in the Learner's Book to assess how well they feel they are able to use an identification key.

Plenary ideas

1 Vertebrate or invertebrate? (5–10 minutes)

Resources: Set of A4 sized cards with pictures of different vertebrates and invertebrates; a set of traffic light cards (one red card, one yellow card, one green card) for each pair of learners.

Description: Show learners the vertebrates/invertebrates cards one at a time. Ask if the animal is a vertebrate or invertebrate. Let pairs of learners decide on their answer. Then ask them to hold up a green card if their answer is 'yes', a red card if their answer is 'no' and a yellow card if they are not sure.

⟩ **Assessment ideas:** Take note of which learners are unsure of answers or give incorrect answers. Spend some time with these learners to find out where their difficulties lie. You could also pair these learners with learners who gave all the correct answers. Then show the cards again and let them help their classmates to understand why the animal is a vertebrate or invertebrate.

2 Correct the sentences (5–10 minutes)

Resources: Copies of sentences for learners, or sentences, written or projected onto the board.

Description: Hand out a copy of the sentences to each learner, or tell learners to copy the sentences from the board.

Learners should underline the words in each sentence that will make the sentence true. Examples of sentences are as follows:

- Birds are vertebrates/invertebrates because they have a backbone/no backbone.
- Insects are vertebrates/invertebrates because they have a backbone/no backbone.
- The hard covering on the body of a crab is called the skeleton/exoskeleton.
- A worm in an invertebrate that has an/no exoskeleton.

⟩ **Assessment ideas:** Ask learners to think about and answer these questions:

- Can I explain the difference between a vertebrate and an invertebrate?
- Do I know what an exoskeleton is?
- Do I know that some invertebrates have an exoskeleton?
- Can I use an identification key?

⟩ **Reflection ideas:** Ask learners to think about these questions:

- What did I find difficult today?
- What things were fun?
- What do I need to practise more?

CROSS-CURRICULAR LINKS

Main teaching ideas 2 and 3 link with criteria for sorting and grouping objects in maths.

Homework ideas

1 Learners could do the Workbook Focus, Practice and Challenge sections for Topic 1.4. Discuss the answers in class and let learners check their own work and make any corrections needed.

2 Learners can take photos or draw pictures of two vertebrates and two invertebrates they observe in or around their homes. They can share their pictures with the class and explain why the animal is a vertebrate or an invertebrate.

Topic worksheets

Worksheet 1.4: Sort and group animals

- This worksheet can be used to reinforce the idea of using observable features to sort and group objects and living things. It is suitable for all learners, but less confident learners may need additional support (see Help sheet) and should answer question 1 only. Most learners should be able to answer questions 2 and 3.
- More confident learners can attempt question 4 on the Stretch sheet.

1.5 Medicines and infectious diseases

LEARNING PLAN

Learning objectives	Learning intention	Success criteria
4Bp.01 Know that medicines can be used to treat some illnesses, and describe how to use them safely.	• To learn why we take medicines. • To be able to describe how to take medicines safely.	• Learners can say why we take medicines. • Learners can describe how to take medicines safely.
4Bp.02 Know that plants and animals can have infectious diseases, and vaccinations can prevent some infectious diseases of animals.	• To find out that plants, animals and people can get infectious diseases. • To learn that vaccinations can prevent some infectious diseases in animals.	• Know that plants, animals and people can get infectious diseases. • Know that vaccinations can prevent some diseases in people and animals.
4TWSc.07 Use secondary information sources to research an answer to a question.	• To find information to answer questions about vaccinations.	• Learners can find information to answer questions about vaccinations.

CONTINUED

Learning objectives	Learning intention	Success criteria
4TWSp.02 Know that there are five main types of scientific enquiry (**research**, fair testing, observing over time, identifying and classifying, and pattern seeking).	• To find scientific information by doing research.	• Learners can find scientific information by doing research.

LANGUAGE SUPPORT

Some of the new words for the topic are used in everyday speech or writing. Give learners the opportunity to use these words correctly by asking them to write or complete sentences using the words. See the examples below.

- **germs** – very tiny living things that can cause diseases, for example we wash our hands before we eat so we don't get germs on our food
- **infect** – when the germs get into your body and make you ill
- **infectious disease** – a disease that is caused by germs

- **instructions** – information that tells us how to do something, for example Ali has a set of instructions to tell him how to build a model car
- **medicines** – substances that we use to help us get better when we are ill, for example cough mixture helps us to stop coughing
- **prevent** – to stop, for example a raincoat prevents us from getting wet when it rains
- **vaccinations** – injections or other medicines that stop us from getting a disease

Common misconceptions

Misconception	How to identify	How to overcome
Plants don't have diseases.	Many learners do not think that plants have the same life processes as animals. Ask learners if they think that plants can have diseases like people and animals do.	Show learners plants or pictures of plants that have been infected with a disease such as rust. Explain that similar kinds of germs cause diseases in plants, animals and humans.

Starter ideas

1 Getting started (5 minutes)

Resources: Learner's Book

Description: Ask learners to look at the picture and silently read the questions in the Learner's Book.

Use the 'Think-pair-share' method to allow learners to think about their answers for a minute or two, then discuss their answer with a partner before sharing their answers with the class

2 Would you take it? (5–10 minutes)

Resources: A selection of images of pills, especially brightly coloured pills, and an image of an unlabelled medicine bottle with liquid inside.

Description: Ask learners to look at the selection of images. How do they know if they are medicines or not? Would they take any of the 'medicines'? Why or why not? Then tell them that they will learn more about taking medicines safely later in the lesson.

Main teaching ideas

1 Think like a scientist 1: How to take medicines safely (40 minutes)

Learning intention: To describe how to take medicines safely

Resources Learner's Book, examples of medicine containers or packaging with instructions on them; Worksheet 1.5 (optional); Digital Classroom Science investigators video: How do people take medicines? (optional)

Description: Read out, or get learners to read out, the instructions on the medicines. Explain that if we follow the instructions the medicines will help us to get better from the illness. Point out that the medicines can be harmful if we do not follow the instructions, for example we take too much of the medicine.

Then ask the learners to read the children's ideas in the Learner's Book about how to take medicines safely. You could get some learners to role play the ideas in the activity. Ask the rest of the class to identify which ideas are right and wrong and to suggest other ideas about taking medicines safely.

Then tell learners to read through the steps in the activity to make sure that they know what they must do. Learners should work in pairs to make their information sheets.

Tell learners that they will be using the the the researching type of scientifc enquiry to find additional information.

Learners could complete Worksheet 1.5 once they've finished the investigation. There is a Help sheet for less confident learners and more confident learners can be challenged to answer the questions on the Stretch sheet.

> **Digital Classroom:** If you have access to the Digital Classroom component, show learners the Science investigators video 'How do people take medicines?' to consolidate their understanding. The i button will explain how to use the video.

> **Differentiation ideas:** Learners who work slower are likely to only include the information in the

Learner's Book to make their information sheets, or you could allow them to complete the task at home.

Faster learners could include additional information and illustrate their information sheets.

> **Assessment ideas:** Check learners' work to make sure that they have identified correct and safe ways to take medicines. Discuss any wrong ideas that you come across and explain why they are not correct.

2 Think like a scientist 2: Research information about vaccinations (10–15 minutes in class to plan, 2–3 days to find information, 20 minutes in class to share findings)

Learning intention: To do research to answer questions about vaccinations; find scientific information by doing research; to find about vaccination programmes in the local area; to find out about the development and use of the first vaccinations

Resources: Learner's Book; access to sources of secondary informations such as reference books and the internet

Description: Read through the instructions in the Learner's Book with the class.

Learners should work in pairs to do their research. Most learners will have been vaccinated against childhood diseases such as polio, measles, mumps and rubella. Many will also have been vaccinated against TB. Learners can ask their parents or caregivers for their vaccination cards to see which diseases they were vaccinated against. They could also visit a local clinic, supervised by an adult, to obtain information about vaccination programmes.

Information on the history of vaccinations is available on the internet.

> **Practical guidance:** Learners may find that some websites say that Edward Jenner first developed a vaccination in the 1770s which was for smallpox. However, there is now evidence that that the first vaccinations were given by the Chinese as early as 1000 CE, also to prevent smallpox. One method used was to make a powder from smallpox scabs. People inhaled the powder. Another method was to scratch matter from a smallpox sore into the skin of another person. This is similar to Jenner's method of vaccination.

Answers about local vaccination programmes will depend on learners' findings. Today most vaccinations are given by injection. However, the vaccinations for polio and rotavirus are given as liquids.

> **Differentiation ideas:** Ask more confident learners to find out what smallpox is and why people are no longer vaccinated for smallpox. (Smallpox is a disease caused by a virus. In the past it killed many people. There have not been any recorded cases of smallpox anywhere since 1977, so health authorities consider it to be have been eradicated. This is why people no longer receive smallpox vaccinations.)

> **Assessment ideas:** Learners can use the checklist to self-assess the work.

How well did I:	I did it very well	I did it quite well	I found it difficult
find information about the first vaccinations?			
find out about which vaccinations are given to children in my local area?			
find out how the different vaccinations are given.			
tell the class about my findings?			

3 Questions about infectious diseases (5–10 minutes)

Learning intention: To learn that plants, animals and people can have infectious diseases; can describe how to take medicines safely

Resources: Learner's Book

Description: Ask learners to name some illnesses or disease they have had. You can prompt them by mentioning common examples such as 'flu and diarrhoea. Discuss in class what an infectious disease is and let learners read about the examples of infectious diseases in plants and animals in the Learner's Book. You could ask proficient readers to read the information to the class. Then let learners answer questions 1–3.

Plenary ideas

1 I can and I know (5 minutes)

Description: Ask learners to each write down three sentences about what they have learnt in the topic. Their sentences should start with either:

I can …

or

I know …

Give learners one or two minutes to write their sentences. Then write or project a list of success criteria onto the board. Learners can compare their sentences with the success criteria to assess if they have grasped the main ideas and skills covered in the topic.

> **Assessment ideas:** This is a self-assessment activity which will help learners to identify areas where they are succeeding or where they need more support.

2 Be the doctor (10 minutes)

Resources: Pretend bottle of pills, filled with sweets (not essential).

Description: Remind learners that they should not take any pills unless they have been told to by a doctor (or their parents have been told to give the pills to them by a doctor). Tell them that the pills you are giving them are pretend pills.

Get learners to role play in pairs. One learner can pretend to be the 'doctor', the other learner is the 'patient'. The 'patient' can tell the 'doctor' that he or she is not feeling well and describe what is wrong with them, e.g. a cough or headache. The 'doctor' then gives the 'patient' the 'pills' and tells him or her how to take the medicine safely. Learners can take turns in different pairs to be the 'doctor' or the 'patient'.

> **Assessment ideas:** Ask each pair: Did the 'doctor' tell you the correct ways to take medicines safely?

> **Reflection ideas:** Ask learners: How have the activities in the topic helped you to know about how take medicines safely?

CROSS-CURRICULAR LINKS

Main teaching idea 1 can be used to practise reading and writing in English.

Main teaching idea 2 can be used to practise data handling and graphing skills in Maths.

Main teaching idea 3 can be used to practise and develop reading skills in English.

Homework ideas

1   Learners can answer questions 1–4 from the
    Learner's Book. All learners should answer
    questions 1–3. Higher-achieving learners should
    answer question 4 as well. Let learners swap
    answers and check one another's work in the next
    lesson under your guidance.

2   Learners could do the Workbook Focus, Practice and
    Challenge sections for Topic 1.5. Discuss the answers
    in class and let learners check their own work.

Topic worksheets

Worksheet 1.5: Different ways to take medicine

This worksheet is suitable for all learners to practise
their data handling and graphing skills. You can
differentiate as follows:

- All learners should be able to answer questions
  1 and 2. The Help sheet will assist learners
  who need more support withdrawing their bar
  charts.

- Most learners should be able to answer
  questions 3 and 4.

- More proficient and confident learners should
  also answer the Stretch questions, 5 and 6.

PROJECT: EARTHWORM FARMING

Part 1:

4SIC.01: Describe how science is used in their local area.

4SIC.05: Discuss how the uses of science can have positive and negative environmental effects on their local area.

Learners should work in pairs to collect their information. They may have to be accompanied by an older sibling or relative.

It may be better to speak to the person in their own language if they do not speak English. Learners can

then translate the information into English. Assist them with this if needed.

Each pair of learners should produce a PowerPoint slide presentation for assessment. An alternative, if they do not have the technology available, is to make a poster.

Learners should present their slide shows to the class. Remind them to talk about each slide, to speak clearly and to look at their audience from time to time (make eye contact).

Assessment for presentation

You can use this assessment rubric to assess learners' presentations:

Criterion	Poor (0–1 mark)	Fair (2–3 marks)	Good (4 marks)	Excellent (5 marks)
Presentation	Poorly prepared. Slides unsuitable, poor quality. Speaker hard to understand/hear. No eye contact.	Some preparation for presentation evident. Slides generally suitable, satisfactory quality. Mostly speaks clearly. Some eye contact.	Prepared for presentation. Suitable slides, good quality. Speaks clearly, easy to hear and understand. Makes sufficient eye contact.	Well prepared for presentation. Relevant slides, excellent quality. Speaks clearly with good use of language. Easy to hear and understand. Good eye contact.
Content	Little information provided for each question.	Answers some of the questions.	Answers all of the questions.	Clear and detailed answers to all questions; additional questions asked and answered.

Challenge question

In which other ways are earthworms useful? Do some research to find out.

Answer

Earthworms make tiny tunnels in the soil. The tunnels help to add air and water to the soil. Plants need air and water to grow well. Having worms in your soil is a good sign that you have a healthy soil.

Find out about other useful invertebrates that people keep: e.g. silkworms for spinning silk, bees for honey.

> 2 Energy

Unit plan

Topic	Approximate number of learning hours	Outline of learning content	Resources
2.1 Energy around us	1.5	• The concept of energy • Knowing that energy is in everything around us • Forms of energy	**Learner's Book:** Think like a scientist: Demonstrate what energy does **Workbook:** Topic 2.1 **Digital Classroom:** Video – Energy around us
2.2 Energy transfers	1.5	• How energy is transferred	**Learner's Book:** Think like a scientist 1: Observe an energy transfer Think like a scientist 2: Plan a fair test on energy transfers Activity: Identify energy transfers **Workbook:** Topic 2.2
2.3 Energy changes	2	• How energy can change form • Knowing that energy cannot be created or destroyed	**Learner's Book:** Think like a scientist: Observe energy changes **Workbook:** Topic 2.3 ⬇ Worksheet 2.3
2.4 Energy and living things	2	• Sources of energy for living things • Energy transfers in food chains	**Learner's Book:** Think like a scientist: Draw food chains **Workbook:** Topic 2.4 ⬇ Worksheet 2.4 ⬇ Unit 2 wordsearch template **Digital Classroom:** Video – Animals need plants for energy Animation – Food chains Song – Food chains

Across unit resources		
Learner's Book:	**Teacher's Resource:**	**Digital Classroom:**
Project – Find out how electricity is made Check your progress quiz	⬇ Language worksheets 1 and 2 ⬇ End of unit test ⬇ Diagnostic check ⬇ Mid-point test ⬇ End -of-year test	End-of-unit quiz

BACKGROUND KNOWLEDGE

Energy is everywhere and in everything. Every time something gets warm, cools down, moves, grows, makes a sound or changes in any way, it uses energy.

Energy is a concept that we are all familiar with. We often use the term energy in everyday life. For example, when we feel tired and don't want to do anything active, we may say we that we have no energy. In Science, energy has a different meaning.

Scientists define energy as the ability to do work. We can think of this as meaning that we need energy to make things happen or change. For example, to make a stationery object such as a ball move, we need to give it energy. The concept of energy is very closely linked to forces which were covered in Stages 1–3. If we apply a force (push or pull) to an object, we give the object more energy. So in the example of a ball, we apply a force when we kick the ball. The force gives the ball energy to move.

All moving things have energy. Learners will probably be able to associate energy with heat and electricity. There is also energy in light and sound. Energy can be stored, such as in food, batteries, or in substances like oil and coal that we use for fuel.

Energy can be transferred from place to place, or object to object. For example, heat and light energy from the Sun are transferred to the Earth. Energy also changes from one form to another. For example, movement energy when we rub our hands together changes to heat energy. But energy cannot be created or destroyed. This principle is known as conservation of energy.

Living things obtain the energy they need for their life processes from their food. The primary source of energy on Earth is the Sun. Plants make their own food using energy from the Sun. Animals eat plants and other animals to obtain the energy they need. We can show the direction of energy transfer from one living thing to another by means of food chains. A food chain is a drawing representing feeding relationships and energy transfers between living things.

TEACHING SKILLS FOCUS

Language awareness

Many learners these days are learning Science in a language that is not their mother tongue. Learners often experience challenges when they learn a subject in an additional language. A teacher who is 'language aware' understands that learners face these difficulties and provides language support to learners.

Because we use language to communicate in teaching Science, every Science lesson is a language lesson. Learning Science is like learning a new language as there are many terms that are used only in Science. Teachers need to be aware that, although learners use scientific terms in speech and writing, this does not mean that they understand them.

It is not only new scientific terms that are challenging for learners. Some everyday words are used in a different way in Science, for example matter, energy and force. This can lead to further difficulties for learners.

When you choose the activities and materials for a lesson, it is important to think about whether learners will have sufficient language skills to make sense of the material and understand what they are required to do. You can support learners in the following ways:

CONTINUED

- Speak slowly and clearly.
- Use drawings, diagrams or other visual materials to explain concepts or provide examples.
- Use physical examples or demonstrations.
- Repeat or say something in a different way using examples that will be familiar to learners.
- Highlight key terms and ask learners to explain them in their own words.

- Provide opportunities for learners to use new language or terms, for example explaining an example to a partner using the new words.
- Introduce new language or terms before setting a task.
- Provide sentence starters or stems for learners when they have to give written answers, for example, *I observed that energy moved from…*, or *I think… because…*

Challenge yourself to include at least one language awareness strategy in each lesson.

2.1 Energy around us

LEARNING PLAN

Learning objectives	Learning intention	Success criteria
4Pf.01 Know that energy is present in all matter and in sound, light and heat.	• To know that energy is in everything around us.	• Learners can identify energy in things around us.
4Pf.03 Know that energy is required for any movement or action to happen.	• To find out that we need energy for any movement or action to happen.	• Learners can demonstrate and explain how energy causes movement.
4TWSp.03 Make a prediction describing some possible outcomes of an enquiry.	• To be able to predict what will happen in an investigation.	• Learners can make a prediction in an investigation.
4TWSa.01 Identify whether results support, or do not support, a prediction.	• To be able to identify if results support, or do not support, the prediction.	• Learners can identify if results support, or do not support, the prediction.

LANGUAGE SUPPORT

Learners will learn and use the following words:

- **energy** – anything that can cause movement or carry out an action. Refer to the notes in the introduction and remind learners that the term has a different meaning in Science to its meaning in everyday life

- **predict** – to say what you think will happen based on what you already know or have observed, for example we can predict that we will burn our hands if we touch a hot stove

Give learners the opportunity to use the words correctly by asking them to write or complete sentences using the words.

Common misconceptions

Misconception	How to identify	How to overcome
Energy is a substance or thing.	Ask learners what they think energy is.	Ask if we can hold or touch energy. Explain that things contain energy and we can see the effects of energy, such as movement, but energy itself is not something made of matter.
Energy is created as the result of movement or another activity, e.g. burning wood in a fire.	Ask learners where energy in a moving ball comes from.	Explain that all energy comes from somewhere. The energy in the ball comes from the person who kicks or throws the ball; the person gets the energy to kick or throw the ball from the food he or she eats.

Starter ideas

1 Getting started (5 minutes)

Resources: Learner's Book

Description: Read the questions in the Learner's Book to the learners. Then use the 'Think-pair-share' method to allow learners to think about their answers for a minute or two, then discuss their answer with a partner before sharing their answers with the class.

This activity will help identify the misconception that energy is a substance or thing.

2 Where does energy come from? (5 minutes)

Resources: Pictures which demonstrate energy in everyday situations or Digital Classroom video: Energy around us (optional)

> **Digital Classroom:** If you have access to the Digital Classroom component, use the video 'Energy around us' to lead a class discussion on what learners know about energy. The i button will explain how to use the video.

Otherwise, show learners the pictures of the different actions.

Ask learners to say where energy comes from for each of the actions (children running or playing – food; food cooking on stove – stove; wind mill turning – wind; washing blowing in wind – wind; mobile phone ringing – cell).

This activity will help to identify the misconception that energy is created as the result of movement or other activity.

Main teaching ideas

1 Be an energy detective (10–15 minutes)

Learning intention: To identify energy in things around us

Resources: Coloured stickers

Description: Explain that we cannot see energy, but we can tell it is there. Ask learners to name some ways they might be able to tell that energy is there. Tell them that this is evidence of energy. Answers could include seeing something move, hearing a sound, seeing light, feeling heat or noticing something change. Ask them to find energy in the classroom. They should put a sticker on anything they think has energy.

Answers: Learners should put stickers on objects such as a phone, food, themselves, a light switch, any electrical item, anything moving such as a dream catcher or mobile, or plants

> **Differentiation ideas:** All learners should be able to do the activity

> **Assessment ideas:** Self-assessment: learners can count the number of things they correctly identified as having energy and rate themselves. For example, 4 or more = good; 2–3 = fair; 0–1: I need help.

2 Think like scientist: Demonstrate what energy does (20 minutes)

Learning intention: To demonstrate and explain how energy causes movement

Resources: Learner's Book; a ping pong ball or ball of crumpled paper for each group

Description: This is a learner-led practical activity. Read through the activity instructions to make sure learners understand what they have to do. You could also demonstrate how they should flick the ball. Learners will be using the observing over time type of scientific enquiry to observe the effect of flicking the ball.

> **Practical guidance:** Let learners work in small groups. They should place the ping pong ball or ball of paper on a flat surface so that it doesn't start rolling on its own. Tell learners to take turns to gently flick the ball and see how far it moves.

Ask learners to predict what will happen if they flick the ball harder. You can write the groups' predictions on the board. Discuss learners' observations at the end of the activity.

> **Differentiation ideas:** Ask more confident learners to suggest a way you can make a second ping pong ball move on the table without flicking it. If there is enough time in the lesson you can allow them to try out their ideas. (They should flick the first ping pong towards the second ball. The energy in the moving ball will make the other ball start to move.)

> **Assessment ideas:** Peer assessment: ask learners to explain to a partner what they have learnt about energy and movement from the practical activity.

3 **Questions from Think like a scientist: Demonstrate what energy does (10–15 minutes)**

Learning intention: To explain how energy causes movement

Resources: Learner's Book

Description: The questions are a follow-up to Think like a scientist. Learners can work on their own or in pairs to answer the questions.

> **Assessment ideas:** Discuss answers in class. Allow learners to check their own work and make any corrections needed.

Plenary ideas

1 **Tell your partner what you have learnt about energy (5 minutes)**

Description: Let learners work in pairs to tell each other three things they have learnt about energy.

> **Assessment ideas:** Self-assessment: Was I able to tell my partner another three things they have learnt about energy?

2 **How am I doing? (2–3 minutes)**

Resources: Self-assessment feature in the Learner's Book.

Description: Let learners think about the Self-assessment questions in the Learner's Book. Their answers will show how learners rate their progress.

> **Assessment ideas:** Self-assessment as described above.

CROSS-CURRICULAR LINKS

Main teaching idea 2 links with measurement in Maths – learners can measure how far the balls travel when they are flicked.

Main teaching idea 3 links with sentence construction and vocabulary in English.

Homework ideas

1 Learners could complete the Workbook Focus, Practice and Challenge sections for Topic 2.1, Discuss answers in class and allow learners to check their own work and correct any errors.

2 Learners can take photos or draw pictures of evidence of energy they observe in or around their homes. They can share their pictures with the class and explain how each picture shows that energy is present.

2.2 Energy transfers

Learning objectives	Learning intention	Success criteria
4Pf.02 Know that energy cannot be made, lost, used up or destroyed but it can be transferred.	• To find out that energy can be transferred from one object to another object. • To be able to observe and describe energy transfer. • To be able to identify energy transfers. • To learn that energy does not get used up or disappear.	• Learners can understand that energy can be transferred from one object to another object. • Learners can observe and describe energy transfer. • Learners can identify energy transfers. • Learners can understand that energy does not get used up or disappear.
4TWSa.03 Make a conclusion from results and relate it to the scientific question being investigated.	• To be able to make a conclusion related to an investigation question.	• Learners can explain observations to make a conclusion related to an investigation question.
4TWSp.01 Ask scientific questions that can be investigated.	• To be able to ask a question that can be investigated.	• Learners can ask a question that can be investigated.
4TWSp.02 Know that there are five main types of scientific enquiry (research, **fair testing**, observing over time, identifying and classifying, and pattern seeking).	• To be able to plan how to use fair testing to answer an investigation question. • To be able to understand why it is important to do fair test investigations.	• Learners can plan a fair test to answer an investigation question. • Learners can say why it is important to do fair test investigations.
4TWSp.04 Identify variables that need to be taken into account when doing a fair test.	• To be able to identify factors that must be the same and factors that will change in a fair test.	• Learners can identify factors that must be the same and factors that will change in a fair test.
4TWSc.04 Describe how repeated measurements and/or observations can give more reliable data.	• To be able to recognise that repeating an investigation makes results more reliable.	• Learners can identify that repeating an investigation makes results more reliable.
4TWSp.05 Identify risks and explain how to stay safe during practical work.	• To be able to identify any safety risks in an investigation and suggest how to stay safe.	• Learners can identify any safety risks in an investigation and suggest how to stay safe.

LANGUAGE SUPPORT

Learners will learn and use the following words:

- **conclusion** – what you have found out from an investigation

- **energy transfer** – when energy moves from one place to another place or from one object to another object

Use the terms whenever possible during the lesson to reinforce them for learners.

Common misconceptions

Misconception	How to identify	How to overcome
Things 'use up' energy, or 'run out of' energy. This misconception is largely due to everyday language and experiences, for example, the cell of a mobile phone going flat, or a person feeling tired and saying they have run out of energy.	Ask learners what happens to the heat energy from a fire when the fire goes out?	Explain that heat energy spreads out or moves in the surroundings. It is still there but spreads out so much that we cannot feel it after a while.

Starter ideas

1   Getting started (5 minutes)

Resources: Learner's Book

Description: Learners should work in pairs to answer the questions. You can ask them to put up their hands to volunteer to share their answers. Choose four or five volunteers to share their answers. Write their answers on the board and discuss them with the class.

2   Feel the heat (10–15 minutes)

Resources: Hot water bottle filled with warm (approx. 30-35°C) water or warmed microwave heat bag

Description: Heat the water to approx. 30-35°C and pour into the hot water bottle, checking that it is not too hot to hold. Do the same if you are using a warmed microwave heat bag.

Get learners to stand in a circle around the classroom or outdoors. Let them pass the hot water bottle or heat bag around the circle so that every learner gets a turn to hold it and pass it on.

Ask learners to describe what they felt when they held the bottle or bag (their hands felt warmer). Ask learners why this happened (the heat energy moved from the hot water bottle or heat bag to their hands).

Ask learners to predict how hot the bag or bottle will feel after half an hour (it will be much cooler). If time permits, do this and let learners feel the bag or bottle again for themselves. Ask: Where did the heat go? (the heat is transferred from the hot bottle or bag into the surroundings).

Some learners may say the hot water bottle or heat bag ran out of heat energy. Point out that their hands felt warm when they held the bag – the heat moved from the bag to their hands. The bag did not run out of heat energy.

Main teaching ideas

1   Think like a scientist 1: Observe an energy transfer (20 minutes)

Learning intentions: To observe and understand that energy moves from one object to another object; to make a conclusion related to investigation question

Resources: Learner's Book; a beaker of hot water, a metal teaspoon, a bead, petroleum jelly, timer or stop-watch (optional)

Description: This can be a learner-led investigation, or you can set it up as a demonstration if you have concerns about learners working with hot water. Learners will be using the observing over time type of scientific enquiry in the activity.

If learners do the activity themselves they should follow the instructions in the Learner's Book. Make sure they are aware of the danger of working with hot water. You should pour the water into the beakers for the learner groups. Hot water from a tap will be warm enough. If you heat water for the activity, it should not be hotter than about 50 degrees C. Learners should then answer questions 3 and 4 in the Learner's Book. You can extend this activity to introduce the idea of repeating measurements to check for measuring errors. Explain that scientists always check their results and usually repeat experiments to make sure they will get the same or similar results. Measurements are reliable if we get the same answer or similar answer each time we repeat a measurement. You could demonstrate this by repeating the investigation two or three times and measuring the time taken for the bead to fall off the spoon each time.

⟩ **Practical guidance:** It should take several minutes for the bead to fall off the spoon, depending on how hot the water is.

⟩ **Differentiation ideas:** You can support learners who struggle with written answers by providing these sentences for them to complete by choosing the correct words:

The bead <u>falls off/stays on</u> the spoon because the petroleum jelly <u>does not melt/melts</u>. This happens becauses the heat energy <u>moves/does not move</u> from the <u>petroleum jelly/hot water</u> to the spoon, which gives the spoon <u>less/more heat</u>. The heat energy from the <u>water/spoon</u> moves to the petroleum jelly and makes it <u>go hard/melt</u>.

2 Moving marbles (10–15 minutes)

Learning intention: To demonstrate and explain that energy is transferred from one object to another object

Resources: Four or five marbles, a ruler with groove in the centre. You could also use a Newton's cradle.

Description: In this activity, learners will observe that movement energy is transferred from one marble to the next marble and then again to the next marble, until it is transferred to the last marble.

You can do this activity as a teacher demonstration if you do not have enough marbles and suitable rulers for a group activity.

⟩ **Practical guidance:** Place the ruler on flat surface with no slope. Place three marbles together in the middle of the ruler. Place one marble at the end of the ruler. Ask learners to predict what they think will happen when you (or they) flick the marble at the end of the ruler. Most learners will say that the marbles in the middle will start to move or roll along the ruler.

Flick the marble and let learners observe what happens (the marble at the far end of the rule ruler will move).

What happens to the marble that was flicked? (it stops).

Ask for ideas why this happened. (The movement energy in the first marble is transferred to the next marble; this made the marble stop as it had passed on its movement energy. That energy was then transferred to the next marble, and so on.)

Repeat the experiment by flicking two marbles at the marbles in the middle of the ruler. Do it again and flick three marbles. Ask learners to identify the pattern

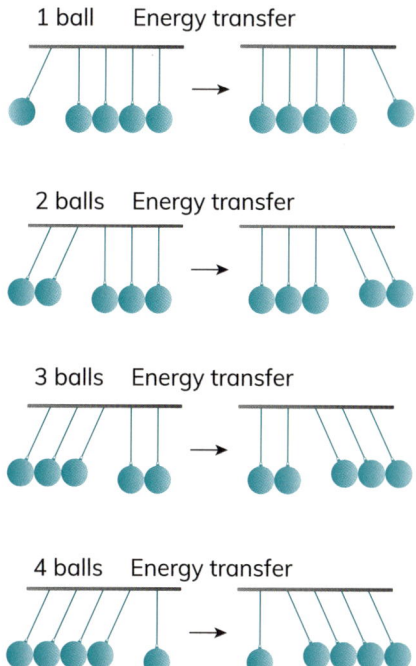

they can observe (the number of marbles that you flick equals the number of marbles that roll away). The drawing shows this pattern in a Newton's cradle.

3 Think like a scientist 2: Plan a fair test on energy transfers (20–30 minutes)

Learning intention: To use fair testing to answer an investigation question

Resources: Learner's Book

Description: Learners can work in pairs or small groups to plan their investigation and answer the question in the Learner's Book. They should discuss Zara's observation which should lead them to ask whether some materials transfer more heat than others. Remind learners that in a fair test there are three things we need to decide on:

- what we will change
- what we will keep the same
- what we will measure.

Learners should be able to explain that repeating observations and measurements will help them check that they have not made any errors in measuring.

⟩ **Differentiation ideas:** More confident learners could carry out the investigation, possibly as a demonstration to the rest of the class. Ask for volunteers to do do this.

⟩ **Assessment ideas:** You can use an assessment rubric, such as the one provided for teacher assessment.

TWS LOs	Beginning	Developing	Mastering
Ask scientific questions to investigate.	Asks a question that may or may not relate to observations.	Asks a question based on observations that may not be testable.	Asks a testable question based on observations.
Identify variables that need to be taken into account when fair testing.	Identifies one or two variables that need to be taken into account in planning a fair test.	Identifies most variables that need to be taken into account in planning a fair test.	Identifies all variables that need to be taken into account in planning a fair test.
Describe how repeated measurements and/or observations can give more reliable data.	Unable to suggest a way to make sure that the results are correctly measured.	With assistance, can suggest a way to make sure that the results are correctly measured.	Can suggest a way to make sure that the results are correctly.
Identify risks and how to stay safe during practical work.	Unable to identify risks and how to stay safe during the investigation.	Needs help to identify risks and how to stay safe during an investigation.	Can identify risks and how to stay safe during an investigation.

Plenary ideas

1 Make sentences about energy transfer (5 minutes)

Resources: Whiteboard or Smartboard

Description: Write or project these words on the board:

1 object - or -moves - one - to - energy - object - transferred - another - is - from

2 disappear - energy - or- get - not – does - used up

Ask learners to rearrange the words to make sentences about what they have learnt about energy transfers.

(1. Energy moves, or is transferred from, one object to another object. 2. Energy does not disappear or get used up.)

> **Assessment ideas:** Self-assessment

- Can I say what an energy transfer is?

- Do I understand that energy does not get used up or disappear?

2 I can and I know (5–10 minutes)

Resources: Learners will need paper and pens or pencils

Description: Ask learners to each write two sentences about what they have learnt in the topic. Their sentences should start with either:

I can …

or

I know …

Give learners one or two few minutes to write their sentences. Then write or project a list of success criteria (from the summary checklist in the Learner's Book) onto the board. Learners can compare their sentences with the success criteria to assess if they have grasped the main ideas and skills covered in the topic.

> **Assessment ideas:** This is a self-assessment activity which will help learners to identify areas where they are succeeding or where they need more support.

CROSS-CURRICULAR LINKS

Plenary activities ideas 1 and 2 link with sentence construction in English.

Homework ideas

1 Learners could complete the Workbook Focus, Practice and Challenge sections for Topic 2.2. In the next lesson, discuss answers. Allow learners to swap answers and check one another's work.

2 Learners should complete the Activity: Identify energy transfers to consolidate their understanding of energy transfers.

Ask more confident learners to suggest two other energy transfers and add them to the table.

In the next lesson, discuss answers. Allow learners check their own work.

2.3 Energy changes

LEARNING PLAN

Learning objectives	Learning intention	Success criteria
4Pf.04 Know that not all energy is transferred from one object to another, but often some energy during a process can be transferred to the surrounding environment and this can be detected as a sound, light or temperature increase.	• To be able to observe that energy can change from one form to a different form. • To be able to find out that some energy moves from an object into the surrounding environment. • To be able to describe energy changes.	• Learners can understand that energy can change from one form of energy to a different form of energy. • Learners can understand that some energy moves from an object into the surrounding environment. • Learners can describe energy changes.
4Pf.02 Know that energy cannot be made, lost, used up or destroyed but it can be transferred.	• To learn that we cannot make energy or destroy energy.	• Learners can understand that we cannot make energy or destroy energy.

LANGUAGE SUPPORT

Make sure that learners understand and can use these terms correctly.

- **destroy** – to make something not exist anymore, for example to destroy a letter by burning it

- **electric appliances** – machines that use electrical energy to make them work, for example washing machines and kettles

- **electrical energy** – the form of energy we get from electricity

Explain the terms. Get learners to make sentences using the words. Their sentences do not have to be scientific.

Common misconceptions

Misconception	How to identify	How to overcome
Energy is truly lost or destroyed in many energy transfers.	Remind learners that all moving things have energy. Ask learners what happens to the energy in a ping pong ball that rolls off a table onto the floor.	Explain that sometimes we see where energy in an object goes, but it is never lost or destroyed, it changes form and may also move into the surroundings.

Misconception	How to identify	How to overcome
		In the case of the falling ping pong ball, some movement energy changes into sound, (we can hear ball hit the floor), some energy changes into heat (we could measure the very small increase in temperature on the floor if we had a sensitive enough thermometer) and some energy is absorbed by the floor.

Starter ideas

1 Getting started (5 minutes)

Resources: Learner's Book

Description: Read through the questions with the class before they answer the questions.

Learners should work in pairs to answer the questions. You can ask them to put up their hands to volunteer to share their answers (for answers, see below).

Ask learners where they think the heat energy their bodies produced comes from. The may say from pedalling/movement.

Then ask where the energy for pedalling came from. They should say from their food.

You can draw an energy chain to show the energy transfers and changes that take place when they ride a bicycle: energy in food → movement energy in legs + heat energy.

Also ask: Where does the heat energy go? (into the surroundings).

Some learners may say that the heat energy given off by their bodies disappears. Point out that the heat energy moves into the surroundings.

2 How does the energy change? (5 minutes)

Description: Get learners to rub their hands together. What change do they notice? (Their hands get warm and made a sound.) Where did the warmth or heat and sound come from? (From rubbing their hands together.)

Ask what sort of energy they used to rub their hands together. How did it change? (Movement changed to heat energy and sound energy.)

Main teaching ideas

1 Think like a scientist: Observe energy changes (20–30 minutes)

Learning intention: To be able to observe and describe energy changes from one form of energy to another form of energy

Resources: Learner's Book; a desk lamp, a paper spiral, some thin string, a pencil, a paper spiral template

Description: In this activity, learners will observe changes over time. Learners should work in small groups and follow the instructions in the Learner's Book. This is a learner-led activity. You could also choose to do a teacher demonstration if you have concerns about learners' safety with using a desk lamp.

You can prepare for the activity by making a paper spiral for each group. If time permits, learners can draw and cut out their own paper spirals. They can use the template in the worksheet pack. They could also colour or decorate their spirals.

> **Practical guidance:** This activity could be learner-led, or a teacher demonstration.

You should use a regular incandescent lamp and not a LED or energy saver lamp as they will not get hot enough. Make sure to hold the paper spiral high enough above the lamp so that it does not touch the lamp and burn.

> **Differentiation ideas:** More confident learners can suggest a way to check that the energy change was from heat energy to movement energy, and not light energy to movement energy, e.g. by holding the spiral above a LED flashlight instead of an incandescent lamp. They should observe whether the spiral turns or not.

> **Assessment ideas:** Learners can write sentences about what they found out about energy changes in the investigation. They can swap sentences with a partner and compare answers. Do they agree on what they have found out?

2 Questions about energy transfers and changes (10–15 minutes)

Learning intention: To identify and describe energy transfer and change

Resources: Learner's Book; pictures of some electrical appliances, such as a stove, a kettle, a toaster and a TV set, to act as stimulus material

Description: After learners have completed the Think like a scientist activity, they can answer the questions on Learner's Book to reinforce their understanding of energy transfers and changes.

You can use the 'Think-pair-share' approach. Let learners answer the questions on their own and then discuss their answers with a partner. Hold a report back session for learners to share their answers in class.

> **Assessment ideas:** Learners can check their own answers and make any corrections or additions needed.

3 Demonstrate energy changes (10–15 minutes)

Learning intention: To identify and describe energy changes

Resources: An elastic band, a piece of paper; Worksheet 2.3 (optional)

Description: Do this activity as a demonstration. Tell the class that we can transfer energy to objects by stretching them or twisting them.

Follow the guideline below to shot shoot a piece of paper with a stretched elastic band.

Ask learners:

1 If they could shoot the elastic band before you stretch it.

2 Why not?

3 To describe the energy changes they observed. (They can do this as an energy chain.)

As a follow-up to reinforce the concept that energy can change form, learners can complete Worksheet 2.3: How far can an elastic band fly?

> **Practical guidance:** Put the elastic band over the end of one finger, pull the band back and let it go so that it flies across the room.

Fold up a small piece of paper into a rectangle. Loop the elastic band over your thumb and forefinger. Place the piece of paper around the elastic band at the point where you would pull the elastic band back to act as a catapult. To shoot the piece of paper, pull on the piece of paper to stretch the elastic band, then let it go.

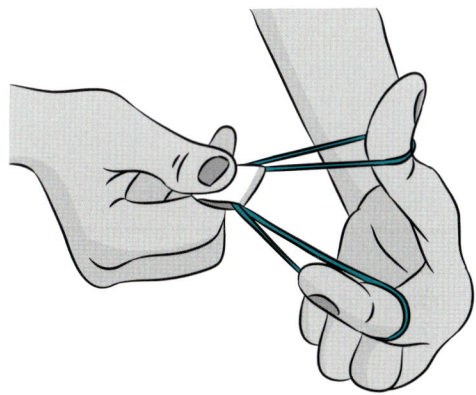

Safety: make sure you aim away from learners, e.g. towards the classroom door.

Answers:

1 No.

2 It does not have energy to move.

3 Learners can describe the energy changes they observed as an energy chain:

movement energy from hand → stored energy in elastic band → movement energy in elastic band and paper.

> **Differentiation ideas:** Learners who need more support to describe energy transfers and changes can use the words given to complete the sentences.

Word list: movement, energy, elastic band, stretched, stored, let go

1 The elastic band got _____ when it was _____.

2 The energy that made the paper fly across the room was _____ in the _____

3 The _____ energy in the elastic band was changed to _____ energy.

Learners can use the words to complete the sentences.

Answers:

1 The elastic band got energy when it was stretched.

2 The energy that made the paper fly across the room was stored in the elastic band.

3 The stored energy in the elastic band was changed to movement energy.

Ask more confident learners to suggest a way they can make the piece of paper fly further. Ask them to explain their answers. (They can stretch the elastic band more – this will give it more stored energy that can changed to movement energy to make the paper fly further.)

Plenary ideas

1 How am I doing? (2–3 minutes)

Resources: Self-assessment feature in Learner's Book

Description: Learners should individually think about the question in the Self-assessment feature. The learners' answers will show how they rate their progress.

2 Quick check (5 minutes)

Description: Let learners stand and quickly say one thing that they have learnt in the topic before sitting down.

> **Assessment ideas:** Learners' answers should give you a quick overview of how well the class has understood the work covered in the topic.

CROSS-CURRICULAR LINKS

Main teaching idea 1 can be linked with Arts and Crafts by letting learners decorate their spiral or make and colour a spiral paper snake.

Homework ideas

1 Learners could answer the questions in the Learner's Book. In the next lesson, discuss answers in class. Allow learners to swap answers and check one another's work.

2 Learners could complete the Workbook Focus, Practice and Challenge sections for Topic 2.3, In the next lesson, discuss answers in class. Allow learners to swap answers and check one another's work.

Topic worksheets

Worksheet 2.3: How far can an elastic band fly?

This practical worksheet is intended to provide practice in measuring length, drawing graphs and in applying knowledge about energy transfers and changes.

All learners should be able to carry steps 1–9. Use the Help sheet for step 5. Learners can use the graph axes template for step 9.

Most learners should be able to answer questions 1, 2 and 3.

More confident learners should complete the additional task and question on the Stretch sheet.

2.4 Energy and living things

Learning objectives	Learning intention	Success criteria
4Bp.03 Know that plants and animals need energy to grow, live and be healthy, and plants get their energy from light while animals get their energy from eating plants or other animals.	• To learn why living things need energy. • To be able to find out where living things get their energy from.	• Learners can say why living things need energy. • Learners can say where living things get their energy from.
4Be.03 Describe food chains as being made of producers and consumers, and classify consumers as herbivores, omnivores, carnivores, predator and/or prey.	• To be able to describe and draw food chains. • To be able to classify consumers as herbivores, omnivores, carnivores, predator and/or prey.	• Learners can describe and draw food chains can classify consumers as herbivores, omnivores, carnivores, predator and/or prey.
4TWSm.02 Use models to show relationships, quantities or scale.	• To know that food chains show the order in which animals eat plants or other animals.	• Learners can say how food chains show the order in which animals eat plants or other animals.
4TWSm.03 Draw a diagram to represent a real-world situation and/or scientific idea.	• To be able to make a food chain drawing to show where animals get their energy from.	• Learners can make a food chain drawing to show where animals get their energy from.

You can make a set of flash cards for learners to use to match the new terms learnt in this topic with their meanings. Write the word on one side of the card and its meaning on the other side. Get learners to test one another.

• **carnivore** – an animal that eats other animals

• **consumer** – a living thing that cannot make its own food and obtain energy by eating other living things, usually an animal that eats plants or other animals

• **food chain** – a drawing that shows the order in which animals eat plants and other animals to get energy

• **herbivore** – an animal that eats plants

• **omnivore** – an animal that eats plants and other animals

• **producer** – a plant that makes its own food using energy from the Sun

• **predator** – an animal that kills and eats other animals

• **prey** – an animal that a predator kills and eats

Some of the key words are used in a different way in everyday life, for example consumer. A consumer is person who buys or uses goods and products. This meaning is, however, similar to the scientific meaning as animals use products (food) from other living things.

Point out the difference in the words 'prey'(an animal that a predators kills and eats) and 'pray' (to speak to the god or gods of your religion). They sound exactly the same and learners may be confused by this. Write both words on the board and explain the difference between them.

Common misconceptions

Misconception	How to identify	How to overcome
Food chain arrows represent who eats whom rather than the flow of energy.	Ask learners why living things eat other living things.	Explain that living things eat other living things in order to get the energy they need to live. A food chain drawing is a way to show the order in which energy passes from one living thing to another in the food it eats.

Starter ideas

1 Why do we need energy? (5–10 minutes)

Resources: Whiteboard or Smartboard

Description: Have a brainstorm session for learners to give examples of why we need energy. Write their answers on the board. Learners will mention movement and some may mention growth. Remind learners that they learnt about some life processes in Stage 3 – nutrition, growth, movement and reproduction. Explain that all living things need energy for their body processes.

2 Getting started (5 minutes)

Resources: Learner's Book

Description: Use the 'Think-pair-share' method to allow learners to think about their answers for a minute or two, then discuss their answer with a partner before sharing their answers with the class.

Look for these answers:

1 To carry out body processes or activities, or similar answer, e.g. to run, play, grow.

2 Yes.

3 From their food.

Main teaching ideas

1 Classify consumers (10–15 minutes)

Learning intention: To explain where living things get their energy from; to be able to classify consumers as herbivores, omnivores, carnivores, predator and/or prey

Resources: Digital Classroom video: Animals need plants for energy (optional), or pictures of a variety of herbivores, omnivores and carnivores feeding

> **Digital Classroom:** If you have access to the Digital Classroom component, use the video 'Animals

need plants for energy' to lead a class discussion about different consumers and where they get their energy – from their food. The i button will explain how to use the video.

Otherwise, show the pictures and ask the class what the animal is eating – a plant or another animal, or both?

Introduce the terms herbivores, omnivores, carnivores, predator and prey.

Reshow the video or pictures and ask learners to classify and group the consumers according to the food they are eating. Also ask learners to identify the predators and the prey animals in the clips.

Answers: From the video: giraffe – herbivore; lion – carnivore; person – omnivore; fish eagle – carnivore; grasshopper – herbivore; frog – carnivore; predators – lion, fish eagle, frog; prey – zebra, fish, insect

---

> **Differentiation ideas:** Ask more confident learners if they think humans are predators. Why or why not?

> **Assessment ideas:** Discuss the answers in class and let learners check their own work and make any corrections that are needed.

Get learners to tell a partner the difference between herbivores, omnivores and carnivores and between predators and prey.

2 Questions about producers and consumers (10 minutes)

Learning intention: To revise understanding of producers and consumers

Resources: Learner's Book

Description: Read the information about on producers and consumers in the Learner's Book. If learners are fluent and confident readers, let them read on their own. You could also pair a fluent and less fluent reader and let them take turns to read the information to each other. Get the more fluent reader to read first. Then let learners answer the questions individually.

> **Assessment ideas:** Discuss answers in class. Learners can check their own work. Ask them to think about why any incorrect answers are wrong.

3 Think like a scientist: Draw food chains (10 minutes)

Learning intention: To describe and draw food chains and identify the order in which animals eat plants or other animals to get their energy

Resources: Learner's Book; Worksheet 2.4 (optional); Digital Classroom animation: Food chains (optional); Digital Classroom song: Food chains (optional)

Description: Explain that we can show the direction in which energy passes in the food that living things eat in a drawing called a food chain.

> **Digital Classroom:** If you have access to the Digital Classroom component, use the animation 'Food chains' to explain how energy is transferred in food chains. The i button will explain how to use the animation.

Use the Digital Classroom song 'Food chains' to recap on energy flow in food chains. The i button will explain how to use the song.

Ask learners if they can draw a food chain of their own.

Remind them of the direction in which the energy moves: plant/producer → herbivore → carnivore.

Then let them draw the food chains in the activity.

Learners could complete Worksheet 2.4 once they've finished the investigation. There is a Help sheet for less confident learners and more confident learners can be challenged to answer the questions on the Stretch sheet.

> **Differentiation ideas:** To support less confident learners, make sets of cards with pictures of different plants and animals. Allow learners to practise making their own simple food chains by putting the cards in the correct order for each food chain.

> **Assessment ideas:** You can assess learner understanding of food chains using this checklist.

Assessment statements:	Tick or cross
The food chains start with a plant/producer	
Consumers in the food chains are in the correct order	
Arrows in food chains point in the correct direction	
Learners can describe energy transfers in a food chain	

Plenary ideas

1 Flash cards (5 minutes)

Resources: Make sets of flash cards for learners, with a new term learnt in this topic on one side of the card and the meanings on the other side.

Description: Use the flash to get learners to test one another. They should read out the meaning of a term to a partner, who must say the term. Learners in the pair can take turns in reading and naming the term. If you only have one set of cards, you can use them for a whole class plenary activity in which you read out the meanings of the terms and ask learners to say the term. Or you say the term and get learners to explain the meaning of the term.

> **Reflection ideas:** Learners should answer the Reflection questions in the Learner's Book.

2 Wordsearch (5 minutes)

Resources: Unit 2 wordsearch template, for each learner. (The answers are highlighted here just for your reference.)

Description: The wordsearch contains key words learnt in the topic. Learners should use the clues to find the words.

Clues

living things get this from their food (energy)

plants get their energy from this (Sun)

living things that cannot make their own food (consumers)

living things that make their own food (producers)

an animal that eats only plants (herbivore)

animals that eat other animals (carnivores)

food for predators (prey)

a drawing that shows how energy moves between living things in their food (food chain)

Answers:

Q	S	E	R	T	U	P	I	O	Y
D	F	G	E	N	E	R	G	Y	H
C	A	R	N	I	V	O	R	E	S
J	K	L	I	A	S	D	D	Z	X
C	F	V	B	U	N	U	M	L	P
E	O	G	B	K	L	C	P	I	T
C	O	N	S	U	M	E	R	S	R
F	D	O	U	P	S	R	E	D	B
C	C	J	N	C	V	S	Y	E	M
V	H	E	R	B	I	V	O	R	E
I	A	A	Y	O	H	K	D	N	W
N	I	R	T	U	J	B	G	I	O
M	N	A	G	Y	T	D	E	F	R

> **Assessment ideas:** Let learners check their own answers and make any corrections needed.

> **Reflection ideas:** Ask learners:

* Was it easy to find the words in the wordsearch?

* Which words were hard to find?

* Were there any words you did not know the meaning of?

* Were there any words you did not know how to spell?

CROSS-CURRICULAR LINKS

Main teaching idea 1 can link with criteria for sorting and grouping data and objects in Maths.

Main teaching idea 2 can link with vocabulary development and sentence construction in English.

Homework ideas

1   Learners can answer the questions about producers and consumers in food chains in the Learner's Book. In the next lesson, discuss answers in class. Allow learners to check and correct their own work.

2   Learners could complete the Workbook Focus, Practice and Challenge sections for Topic 2.4, In the next lesson, discuss answers in class. Allow learners to swap answers and check one another's work.

Topic worksheets

Worksheet 2.4: Make food chains

This worksheet is intended to consolidate learners' understanding of food chains and give them practice in drawing food chains.

Most learners should be able to answer questions 1–4.

More confident learners should attempt the stretch questions, 5 and 6.

PROJECT: FIND OUT HOW ELECTRICITY IS MADE

Part 1: How electricity is made in my area

4SIC.02 Describe how science is used in my local area

Learners should work in pairs. They will need to speak to people in their local authority or do some research on the internet to find out how electricity is made. They should use the list of questions to guide their research.

Learners should present their information in a poster or information sheet with drawings or photos.

Learners should display their posters in the classroom for peer-assessment purposes. Make copies of the assessment sheet for learners.

Information sheet peer assessment

Learners should use the grid below for peer assessment. They should tick the boxes on the grid to let their classmate know what they thought about their electricity information sheet or poster.

How well did _____:	Very well	Quite well	Not well
use pictures and information to explain how electricity is made in your area?			
make the information sheet or poster look nice?			
show the energy changes that happen when electricity is made?			
explain how we get electricity in our homes?			

Part 2: Discussion

Science in Context objective: Discuss how the uses of science can have positive and negative environmental effects on my local area.

Have a class discussion about the main source of energy used for making electricity in your area. Talk about whether or not the energy source pollutes the environment or has any other harmful effects. For example:

- Making electricity from coal uses huge amounts of water and also creates air pollution.
- Making solar electricity needs large areas of land for the solar panels. This could destroy or damage the habitats of plants and animals.
- Hydro-electricity affects the flow of rivers and the plants and animals that live in and around the rivers.
- Wind farms endanger flying animals such as bats and birds.

Does it have any positive effects on the environment? For example, solar electricity and wind powered electricity do not create air pollution.

Get learners to write one or two sentences as a conclusion for the discussion.

⟩3 Materials

Unit plan

Topic	Approximate number of learning hours	Outline of learning content	Resources
3.1 Materials, substances and particles	2	• Review prior knowledge about materials • Introduce idea of all materials/substances being made of particles • Describe the particle model for solids and liquids	**Learner's Book:** Think like a scientist: Demonstrate that particles of liquids move Activity: Play the particle game **Workbook:** Topic 3.1 ⤓ Worksheet 3.1 **Digital Classroom:** Animation – Matter is made of particles
3.2 How do solids and liquids behave?	2	• Demonstrate how it is very difficult to change the shape of solid objects such as chairs • Investigate question to see if water can change its shape Observe and explain behaviour of powders	**Learner's Book:** Think like a scientist 1: Plan an investigation about changing the shape of water Think like a scientist 2: Investigate solids that can flow **Workbook:** Topic 3.2 ⤓ Worksheet 3.2 **Digital Classroom:** Video – Properties of solids and liquids
3.3 Melting and solidifying	2	• Change of state in melting and solidifying • Demonstrate solids melting and comparing rates at which different solids melt	**Learner's Book:** Think like a scientist 1: What happens to ice when it is heated? Think like a scientist 2: Compare melting in different solids **Workbook:** Topic 3.3 ⤓ Worksheets 3.3A, 3.3B and 3.3C **Digital Classroom:** Science Investigators video – Do some solids melt more quickly than others?

Topic	Approximate number of learning hours	Outline of learning content	Resources
3.4 Chemical reactions	3	• Chemical reactions make new substances form • Observation and explanation of rusting in wire wool • Demonstration of a chemical reaction	**Learner's Book:** Think like a scientist: Which substances react to form rust? Activity: How can we prevent rusting? **Workbook:** Topic 3.4 ⬇ Worksheet 3.4

Across unit resources

Learner's Book:

Project: Frozen foods

Check your progress quiz

Teacher's Resource:

⬇ Language worksheets 1 & 2

⬇ End-of-unit test

⬇ Diagnostic check

⬇ Mid-point test

⬇ End-of-year test

Digital Classroom:

End-of-unit quiz

BACKGROUND KNOWLEDGE

The main ideas for this unit are that:

- all substances and materials are made of very small particles which are always moving

- substances and materials exist in different states, either as a solid, a liquid or a gas

- substances can change state if they are heated or cooled enough and that these changes are physical changes which do not change the substance into another substance

- chemical reactions cause new substances to form.

To explain the solid, liquid and gas states of substances, we use the particle model.

The three main points of the particle model can be summarised as follows.

1 All matter is made up of particles.

2 The particles are in constant motion.

3 The particles are attracted towards one another.

Some of your learners may ask you what the particles in substances are made of. Tell them that in a bar of gold the particles are gold, in water the particles are water. Each substance is made up of very small particles that we can't see even under a microscope – these are atoms and molecules that they will learn about later in at Secondary School level.

CONTINUED

The particle model can be used to help explain the properties of solids, liquids and gases and changes of state. For example, solids and liquids are very difficult to compress (squash) as the particles are close together.

Temperature is a measure of the average kinetic energy (movement energy) of the particles in a substance. Adding heat energy speeds up the particles as some of the heat energy changes into movement energy. We can detect the addition of heat energy by an increase in temperature.
The faster the particles are moving, the higher the temperature. This principle also applies to the loss of heat, or cooling. Particles slow down when they are cooled. The slower the particles are moving, the lower the temperature. The amount of movement energy that the particles have affects the state of substances.

During a change of state, such as melting or solidifying, the particles of the substance either gain heat and move faster (melting), or lose heat and move slower (solidifying). In a solid there are forces that hold the particles tightly together. The particles are able to vibrate in fixed position, but they cannot move freely. To melt a solid, energy is required to overcome the forces of attraction between the particles and allow the particles to pull away from each other. The energy is provided when the solid is heated. At this point the solid melts to form a liquid. Although the particles are still loosely connected, they are able to move around. Note that not all solids melt when they are heated. Some solids may undergo chemical changes as a result of heating. For example, paper burns rather than melts. Burning is a chemical reaction in which substances react with oxygen gas in the air when they are heated to form new substances such as carbon dioxide.

Some learners may think that heating any substance will change it into a new substance. This misconception may be due to observations involving heating, such as baking a cake, or burning paper or wood.

In solidifying, the particles in a liquid that is cooled lose energy. The particles slow down and move closer together. If the particles are cooled enough, they move close enough to be pulled back together by the forces of attraction between them. The liquid then solidifies and becomes a solid. Note that freezing, such as when water turns to ice, is a form of solidifying. But not all liquids need to be put in a freezer or cooled to a very low temperature to change to solids. This is why is it is better to use the term 'solidifying' rather than 'freezing'.

Because of a focus on water when doing most of the change of state activities (as water is a safe substance to use), learners sometimes assume that it is only water that can change state. Try to use other examples when teaching this content, for example you could melt butter and chocolate, as in Think like a scientist 2 in Topic 3.3, or you could freeze cooking oil or vinegar.

During a change of state there is no change to the particles themselves. The particles in the liquid state are same as the particles in the solid state, but they have more energy. The opposite is also true – the particles in the solid state are same as the particles in the liquid state but they have less energy. This means that when a substance changes state, there is no chemical change to the substance, only a physical change in its form.

Chemical changes occur when two or more substances react with one another other to form a new substance. This is called a chemical reaction. Chemical reactions happen around us, for example when we bake a cake or when milk or fruit juice goes sour. There are different ways to tell if a chemical reaction has taken pace. They include a change in colour, a change in temperature and gas being given off. Learners will explore the evidence for chemical reactions further in Stage 6.

TEACHING SKILLS FOCUS

Peer learning

Peer learning is another form of active learning. Peer learning refers to learners learning with and from each other. Explaining or demonstrating something to someone else helps to reinforce the concept, skill or information in your own mind. In peer learning, learners improve their own learning when they explain their ideas to others and take part in activities in which they can learn from their peers. In this way, peer learning helps learners to take responsibility for their own learning.

Some learners may feel too shy or embarrassed to tell their teacher that they are struggling or do not understand something. Learners often feel more comfortable and open when interacting with a peer. Peer learning thus leads to more open discussion and encourages learners to give their own ideas and opinions. Peer learning is a non-threatening way for learners to express any difficulties they are having in understanding the work. It can be a useful strategy in mixed ability groups where less confident learners can learn from and be assisted by more confident learners.

Using peer learning strategies also allows the teacher to find out more about learners' understanding of a concept or learning material.

The 'Think-pair-share' activities suggested in the notes for Units 1 and 2 are an example of peer learning. Here are some other ideas for using peer learning in your classroom:

- Get learners to ask each other questions about what they have learned.
- Peer teaching, in which learners explain or demonstrate to one another what they have learned. For example, learners could show their peers how they draw bar graphs.
- In the 'Think aloud and write' technique, one learner thinks out loud while their partner writes down the answer or ideas for them, giving them praise or corrections. Learners can then swap roles for another question. This strategy is useful because voicing their thinking helps learners to get a better understanding of their own learning and thought processes (metacognition). It also encourages them to use scientific vocabulary.
- In group work, encourage learners to help each other if they do not understand a question, problem or idea.

Assessing peer learning

- Use verbal feedback during group work. Walk around the room, check in with each group, ask for questions and listen to the group. Assist if needed by clarifying explanations or asking for information from learners.
- Have quick report-backs by groups to the class on what they have learnt or discussed.

As a challenge, try to include at least one peer learning opportunity in each lesson.

3.1 Materials, substances and particles

LEARNING PLAN

Learning objectives	Learning intention	Success criteria
4Cm.01 Describe the particle model for solids and liquids.	• To learn that the particle model describes the differences between substances that are solids, liquids and gases. • To be able to describe the particle model for solids and liquids.	• Learners can understand that the particle model describes the differences between substances that are solids, liquids and gases. • Learners can describe the particle model for solids and liquids.

CONTINUED

Learning objectives	Learning intention	Success criteria
4Cm.02 Understand the difference between materials, substances and particles.	• To be able to find out the difference between materials, substances and particles.	• Learners understand the difference between materials, substances and particles.
4Cm.03 Know that particles are in constant motion, even when in a solid.	• To be able to show that particles move all the time. • To play a game to demonstrate movement in solids and liquids.	• Learners know that particles move all the time. • Learners can demonstrate in a game movement in solids and liquids.
4TWSm.03 Draw a diagram to represent a real-world situation and/or scientific idea.	• To be able to draw observations to show that particles are moving.	• Learners can make a drawing to show movement of particles in a liquid.
4TWSc.08 Collect and record observations and/or measurements in tables and diagrams.	• To be able to record observations in a diagram of moving particles.	• Learners can record observations in a diagram of moving particles.
4TWSm.02 Use models to show relationships, quantities or scale.	• To play a game to demonstrate how solids and liquids are different.	• Learners can say how a game can demonstrate in a game how solids and liquids are different.

LANGUAGE SUPPORT

Use everyday examples to explain the meanings of these words used in the topic: compare, material, particle, substance.

- **compare** – to look at two or more things and say what is the same about them and what is different
- **material** – kinds of matter that we use, such glass and metal
- **particle** – a very small part or bit of something
- **substance** – a particular type of solid, liquid or gas, for example water

For example, concrete is a material we use for building. Concrete is made of other substances, such as cement powder, water and sand. Sand is made of small grains or particles.

Ask a tall girl learner to stand next to a shorter girl learner. Ask the class to say who is taller and who shorter. Tell them that they have compared the height of the two learners. Explain that we also look at things that are similar when we compare, for example both learners are girls.

Common misconceptions

Misconception	How to identify	How to overcome
There is air between particles in solids and liquids.	Ask learners to draw picture of a solid, e.g. an eraser. Ask them to label the drawing. Ask them where there is air in the drawing. The only air is around the eraser.	Explain that air is also made of particles. Then tell learners that the spaces between particles in a solid (or a liquid) are so small that other particles cannot fit between them, so there is nothing in the spaces.

Starter ideas

1 Getting started (5 minutes)

Resources: Learner's Book; materials in the classroom – try to include a bottle or glass of water and a fizzy drink that you open to release the carbon dioxide gas.

Description: Read the questions in the Learner's Book to the learners. Then use the 'Think-pair-share' method to allow learners to think about their answers for a minute or two, then discuss their answer with a partner before sharing their answers with the class.

You can follow up by asking how learners they decided if each material is a solid, a liquid or a gas. Expect the following kinds of answers:

'I know it's a solid if it's hard' or 'I know it's a liquid if it's wet' or 'I know it's a gas if I can't see it'.

2 Is it a solid, a liquid or a gas? (5 minutes)

Resources: A glass of water, a balloon, a stone, a bubble wand and bubble mixture, or pictures if you do not have access to these items

Description: Show the class the materials. Ask learners to say which materials are solid (glass, balloon, stone, bubble wand) and which liquid (water, bubble mixture). Ask if there are gases present (air around us). Then blow up the balloon and make bubbles with the bubble wand. Ask learners what makes the balloon blow up and the bubbles form (gas/air). Remind them that air is a gas that is all around us.

Main teaching ideas

1 Think like a scientist: Demonstrate that particles of liquids move (20 minutes)

Learning intention: To show that particles in a liquid move all the time

Resources: Learner's Book, per group: one beaker or glass jar, water, liquid food dye or colouring, a measuring spoon or measuring cup

Description: Read through the instructions with learners so that they know what they must do. Learners will use the observing changes over time type of scientific enquiry.

Learners should observe that the food dye colour spreads through the water without being stirred. This demonstrates that particles can move on their own.

> **Practical guidance:** This is a learner-led activity.

Let learners work in groups of four or five.

Make sure that learners do not stir the water in the beaker or move the beaker in any way.

> **Differentiation ideas:** Ask more confident learners to predict what would happen if they put the food dye into warm water (the colour spreads faster). If time permits, they can find out for themselves. In this case, provide beakers of warm water for learners.

> **Assessment ideas:** Learners can work in pairs to explain to a partner how their drawing shows that particles move on their own.

2 Make a particle model (15–20 minutes)

Learning intention: To demonstrate the difference in the arrangement of particles in solids and liquids

Resources: Play dough or modelling clay

Description: Let learners work in pairs.

Make 12 small same-sized balls of play dough or modelling clay for each pair of learners, or let learners make their own balls.

Tell the class that the balls are particles. Ask the pairs to arrange the 'particles' to make a model of a solid and of a liquid. They should use half of the 'particles' in each model.

Answers: Learners can look at the pictures of the particle model for solids and liquids in the Learner's Book to guide them.

> **Assessment ideas:** Learners can tell another pair about how their models show of the arrangement of particles in solids and liquids.

3 Activity: Play the particle game (10 minutes)

Learning intention: To use a game to demonstrate the relationship between the arrangement and movement of particles in solids and liquids

Resources: Learner's Book; Worksheet 3.1 (optional); Digital Classroom animation: Matter is made of particles (optional)

Description: Give the learners the instructions for how they must behave as solid particles, as listed in the Learner's Book. Note that you need to be aware of cultural sensitivities here because touching other learners may not be appropriate in some cultures.

> **Practical guidance:** You will need to have a big empty space to do this activity (outside in the school yard or a netball or basketball court would be good). If you have to do the activity indoors, use the school hall or gym. It will be noisy though, so outside is much better.

Divide the class into groups of 10–15 learners. Tell the learners that each person represents a particle, and that they are going to pretend to be solid particles, then liquid particles.

Learners should pretend to be solid particles. They should stand close together in rows. They link arms tightly with their neighbours. The learners at the ends of each row should hold tightly to the shoulders of the person in front of them.

After a minute or so, stop the groups to get their attention.

Learners should next pretend to be liquid particles by unlinking their arms. They should spread out until they are just holding hands. They should move around as much as they can without letting go of each other's hands.

Learners should answer questions 1–4 from the Learner's Book. Learners could also complete Worksheet 3.1. There is a Help sheet that can be given to less confident learners. More confident learners can be challenged to complete the extra questions on the Stretch sheet.

> **Digital Classroom:** If you have access to the Digital Classroom component, use the animation 'Matter is made of particles' to reinforce the concept that matter is made of particles. The i button will explain how to use the animation.

> **Assessment ideas:** Refer to the 'How am I doing?' feature in the Learner's Book.

Plenary ideas

1 Solids and liquids traffic lights (5–10 minutes)

Resources: Sets of red, yellow and green traffic light cards, one set for each learner

Description: Each learner should have a red, yellow and green card. Call out some statements about the particle model for solids and liquids. Here are some examples:

- There are spaces between the particles.
- The particles move very little.
- The particles are quite close together.
- The particles are very close together.
- The particles can slide past each other.
- The particles are arranged in a regular pattern.

Learners should hold up the green card if they know whether the statement refers to a solid or a liquid, or both; the yellow card if they are not sure; and a red card if they don't know the answer. Learners' responses with yellow and red cards should give you an idea of which learners need some additional support for this topic.

> **Reflection ideas:** Ask learners: How did the activities in the topic help you understand the particle model?

2 How am I doing? (2–3 minutes)

Resources: Self-assessment feature

Description: Learners should individually think about the questions in the Self-assessment feature. Learners' answers will show how they rate their progress in understanding the particle model.

CROSS-CURRICULAR LINKS

Main teaching idea 2 can be linked with division in Maths as learners have to halve their 12 play dough balls into two sets of six.

Homework ideas

1   Learners can answer the questions in the Learner's Book about materials, particles and substances. In the next lesson, discuss answers in class. Allow learners to swap answers and check one another's work.

2 Learners could complete the Workbook Focus, Practice and Challenge sections for Topic 3.1. In the next lesson, discuss answers in class. Allow learners to swap answers and check one another's work.

Topic worksheets

Worksheet 3.1: Make a particle model

This worksheet is intended to consolidate learners' understanding of the particle model of matter for solids and liquids.

All learners should be able to answer question 1. The Help sheet will assist learners who need more support.

More confident learners can answer the Stretch questions 2 and 3 of the worksheet in which they compare the arrangement and movement of particles in solids and liquids.

3.2 How do solids and liquids behave?

LEARNING PLAN

Learning objectives	Learning intention	Success criteria
4Cp.01 Use the particle model to explain the properties of solids and liquids. 4Cp.02 Describe and explain how some solids can behave like liquids (e.g. powders), referring to the particle model.	• To be able to use the particle model to explain how solids and liquids behave. • To be able to describe and explain how some solids can behave like liquids.	• Learners can use the particle model to explain how solids and liquids behave. • Learners can describe and explain how some solids can behave like liquids.
4TLp.01 Ask scientific questions that can be investigated.	• To be able to ask a question to investigate.	• Learners can ask a question that can be investigated.
4TWSc.03 Choose equipment from a provided selection and use it appropriately.	• To be able to choose which equipment to use in an investigation.	• Learners can choose which equipment to use in an investigation.
4TWSm.03 Draw a diagram to represent a real-world situation and/or scientific idea.	• To be able to draw a picture of observations.	• Learners can draw a picture of observations.
4TWSa.03 Make a conclusion from results and relate it to the scientific question being investigated.	• To be able to write a conclusion about observations.	• Learners can write a conclusion about observations.
4TWSc.08 Collect and record observations and/or measurements in tables and diagrams.	• To be able to collect and record measurements in a table. • To be able to draw pictures of observations	• Learners can collect and record measurements in a table. • Learners can draw pictures of observations.

CONTINUED

Learning objectives	Learning intention	Success criteria
4TWSc.04 Describe how repeated measurements and/or observations can give more reliable data.	• To be able to say how to make sure measurements are reliable.	• Learners can say how to make sure measurements are reliable.
4TWSc.05 Take measurements in standard units, describing the advantage of standard units over non-standard units.	• To be able to measure time.	• Learners can measure time.
4TSWa.04 Present and interpret results using tables, bar charts and dot plots.	• To be able to draw a bar chart of results.	• Learners can draw a bar chart of results.
4TWSa.02 Describe simple patterns in results.	• To be able to describe a pattern in results.	• Learners can describe a pattern in results.
4TWSp.02 Know that there are five main types of scientific enquiry (research, fair testing, observing over time, identifying and classifying, and **pattern seeking**).	• To think about how we can use patterns in results in other investigations.	• Learners can say how we can use patterns in results in other investigations.

LANGUAGE SUPPORT

The new words for this topic are: pour, property, powder

- **pour** – to make a liquid or other substance flow out of or into a container. For example, Atul pours water from the jug into a glass.

- **property** – what a substance or material is like, or the way it behaves. For example, a property of rock is that is hard. A property of elastic is that it can stretch. Another example of a property is building or a piece of land. Explain that this is not the same as a property of a material.

- **powder** – a solid with fine grains that have air spaces between them, such as baby powder or flour.

Remind learners they have learnt about properties of materials in Stage 2. Revise the definitions with learners and ask them to name some properties of materials, e.g. they are hard, shiny, waterproof.

Common misconceptions

Misconception	How to identify	How to overcome
All liquids have water in them.	Show learner pictures of examples of different liquids such as shampoo, cooking oil, fruit juice and syrup. Ask them if they are all liquids. If not, why not?	Explain that water is the liquid that we are all familiar with, but that any substance that can be poured or can flow is a liquid. Some liquids are thicker than others and they will pour more slowly, e.g. syrup.

Starter ideas

1 Getting started (5 minutes)

Resources: Learner's Book

Description: Read the questions to the class. Ask learners to raise their hands if they think the statement is true and keep their hands down if it is false.

The show of hands for each statement will help you to see which learners need some additional support in recognising the main features of the particle model.

2 Is it a solid or a liquid? (5–10 minutes)

Resources: Examples or pictures of some solids and liquids, such as a bottle of cooking oil, a stone, flour, ice cream, water; Digital Classroom video: Properties of solids and liquids (optional)

> **Digital Classroom:** If you have access to the Digital Classroom component, use the video 'Properties of solids and liquids' to consolidate learners' understanding of the properties of solids and liquids. The i button will explain how to use the video.

Show the pictures or samples to learners. Ask them to decide in pairs if each picture or sample shows a solid or liquid, or both (e.g. solid bottle, liquid cooking oil). Then ask how they decided if it was solid or liquid. Learners should identify properties of the material or substance which they think make it a solid or a liquid, e.g. a stone is a solid because it is hard. Pairs can report back on their answers.

Don't be concerned about unscientific answers, the purpose is to stimulate thinking about properties of solids and liquids.

Main teaching ideas

1 Think like a scientist 1: Plan an investigation about changing the shape of water (25 minutes)

Learning intention: To plan an investigation to identify properties of liquids

Resources: Digital Classroom video: Properties of solids and liquids (optional), Learner's Book. Each group will need water and containers of different shapes and sizes, such as a drinking glass, square lunchbox, glass bowl, clear plastic bag, saucer, measuring jug or measuring cylinder. Also put out some equipment which is not needed, such as thermometers, cardboard boxes and timers.

Description: Tell learners to look at the stimulus picture in the Learner's Book. Explain that they are going to plan an investigation to find out which of the girls in the picture is correct.

Read through the instructions for the activity to make sure that learners understand what they need to do.

Learners need choose from a range of equipment, so put out some equipment that is not suitable or necessary along with the relevant equipment.

> **Digital Classroom:** If you have access to the Digital Classroom component, use the video 'Properties of solids and liquids' to lead a discussion on solids and liquids. The i button will explain how to use the video.

> **Practical guidance:** This is a learner-led investigation.

Give the learners ten minutes to discuss what they are going to do.

Walk around the class and find out what they have decided.

Put out all the equipment on the front table for learners to choose from.

They should be able to demonstrate that the water takes on the shape of the container when they pour the water into the different shaped containers.

At the end of the activity, discuss what learners have found out about the properties of water. Ask them how they can use the investigation they planned to find out if all liquids behave in the same way. Repeat the investigation using different liquids.

> **Differentiation ideas:** More confident learners could plan and carry out an investigation to find out which liquids change shape or flow the quickest, e.g. oil, liquid soap, water, syrup.

> **Assessment ideas:** You can use this checklist to assess learners investigations:

Were learners able to:	Yes	Needed help
ask a question to investigate?		
choose which equipment to use?		
use the equipment correctly?		
record their observations in drawings?		
make a conclusion from their observations which is related to the question investigated?		

2 Can solids flow? (10 minutes)

Learning intention: To demonstrate that small particles of solids can flow

Resources: Learner's Book; a re-sealable plastic bag, rolling pin, wooden mallet or glass bottle, a cookie, jar or beaker

Description: This is a teacher demonstration.

Show learners the cookie. Ask them if it is solid or a liquid. Ask for some properties of the cookie. Look for these answers: it is hard, it cannot change shape, it cannot flow or be poured.

Ask the class if it is possible to make the biscuit behave like a liquid. Then demonstrate that by crushing the biscuit you can make it act like liquid.

> **Practical guidance:** Put the biscuit into the plastic bag and seal the bag. Use the rolling pin, wooden mallet or glass bottle to crush the biscuit into small pieces.

Hold up the bag with the crushed biscuit. Ask these questions:

Has the biscuit changed shape? (Yes)

Is it still hard? (Yes, the pieces are hard)

Is the biscuit still a solid? (Yes)

Then open the bag and pour the crushed biscuit into a jar or beaker.

Ask:

Can we pour the biscuit? (Yes)

Is this a property of a solid or a liquid? (Liquid)

How did we make the solid pour like a liquid? (Crushed it into small pieces)

3 Think like a scientist 2: Investigate solids that can flow (30–40 minutes)

Learning intention: To measure the time it takes for different solids to be poured.

Resources: Learner's Book. Per group: filter funnel (or clear 500 ml plastic water bottle, scissors, permanent marker), measuring cup or cylinder, beaker or jar, salt, sugar, flour and sand, timer, magnifying glass, paper, Worksheet 3.2 (optional).

You can make your own funnel using a clear 500 ml plastic water bottle, scissors, and a marking pen.

Description: Ask learners to read through the instructions in the Learner's Book. Tell them to ask you about anything they are not sure of before they start the activity. Make sure that learners know that they need to repeat the test with each solid. If you are short of time, you can get each group to test a different solid.

Explain to learners how to look for a pattern in their results. We see a pattern when we get the same results in predictable way. For example, if we see that when we melt ice cubes in our hand, bigger ice cubes always take longer to melt than smaller ice cubes.

Discuss the units of time learners will use. Remind them that the standard unit of time is the second. If they don't have a timer that can measure time in seconds, how else can they measure seconds? One way is to count 1001, 1002, 1003, and so on. Talk about why this method is not accurate. For example, some people will count faster or slower than others. Also point that often we cannot compare our results with other people's if we use non-standard units.

Hold a short report-back session for groups to share their findings with the class.

Learners can complete Worksheet 3.2 once they've finished the investigation. There is a Help sheet for less confident learners and Stretch sheet to challenge more confident learners.

> **Practical guidance:** This is a learner-led activity. Learners should work in groups of four or five.

You can make your own funnel using a clear 500 ml plastic water bottle, scissors and a marking pen. Take the lid off the bottle. Draw a line around the middle of the bottle with a marking pen. Cut the bottle in half along the line. The top half of the bottle is your funnel. Make as many as you need for the number of groups of learners in your class.

If you are short of time, you can get each group to test a different solid.

> **Differentiation ideas:** More confident learners can repeat the investigation with other solids, e.g. rice or cereals.

> **Assessment ideas:** Learners can assess their own performance in the activity.

How well was I able to:	Very well	Okay	I needed help
follow the instructions?			
measure the time taken for the solids to flow?			
record results in a table?			
draw a graph of the results?			
identify a pattern in the results?			

Plenary ideas

1 I can and I know (5–10 minutes)

Resources: Learners will need paper and pens or pencils

Description: Ask learners to each write two sentences about what they have learnt in the topic. Their sentences should start with either:

I can…

or

I know…

Give learners one or two minutes to write their sentences. Then write or project a list of success criteria onto the board. Learners can compare their sentences with the success criteria to assess if they have understood the main ideas and skills covered in the topic.

> **Assessment ideas:** This is a self-assessment activity which will help learners to identify areas where they are succeeding or where they need more support.

2 How am I doing? (2–3 minutes)

Resources: Self-assessment feature in the Learner's Book.

Description: Learners should individually think about the questions in the Self-assessment feature. Learners' answers will show how they rate their progress in being able to use the particle model to explain the properties of solids and liquids.

CROSS-CURRICULAR LINKS

The recording of results in a table and drawing a graph in main teaching idea 3 link with data handling and graphing in Maths.

Homework ideas

1   Learners could complete the Workbook Focus, Practice and Challenge sections for Topic 3.2. In the next lesson, discuss answers in class. Allow learners to check their own work.

2   Ask learners to make a table, such as the one shown below, in which they compare solids and liquids and powders.

	Solid	Liquid	Powder
Drawing to show how particles are arranged			
Does it have fixed shape?			
Can it be squashed?			
Can you pour it?			
Example			

In the next lesson, discuss answers in class. Learners can swap tables with a partner and check one another's work.

Topic worksheets

Worksheet 3.2: Make a sand clock

This practical worksheet is an application of the concept that some solids can flow. Learners will make a sand clock. The worksheet can used for differentiation as follows.

Learners who need more support can use the Help sheet to assist them in making their sand clock. Other learners can discuss and devise their own method using the materials provided. More confident learners can modify their sand clock design to make one that can measure a specific length of time, as outlined in Stretch question 4.

Most learners should be able to answer questions 1–3.

More confident learners can answer Stretch questions 4 and 5.

3.3 Melting and solidifying

LEARNING PLAN

Learning objectives	Learning intention	Success criteria
4Cc.01 Describe solidification/ freezing and melting, using the particle model to describe the change of state.	• To be able to describe melting and solidifying. To be able to use the particle model to describe change of state.	• Learners can describe melting and solidifying. Learners can use the particle model to describe change of state.
4Cc.02 Understand that the change of state of a substance is a physical process.	• To learn that change of state is a physical process that does not change the type of substance.	• Learners can understand that a change of state is a physical process that does not change the type of substance.
4TWSp.03 Make a prediction describing some possible outcomes of an enquiry.	• To be able to make a prediction for an investigation.	• Learners can make a prediction for an investigation.
4TWSp.04 Identify variables that need to be taken into account when doing a fair test.	• To be able to identify factors in a fair test.	• Learners can identify factors in a fair test.

LANGUAGE SUPPORT

Make sure that learners understand the meanings of the following words:

- **change of state** – when materials and substances change from one form to another when they are heated or cooled

- **melting** – when a solid changes state to become a liquid

- **physical process** – when a substance changes form, e.g. melts, but does not become a new substance

- **solidifying** – when a liquid changes state to become a solid

Ask learners to write sentences in they which they use the words. You could give them sentence stems such as:

- An example of a change of state is…

- Melting happens when…

- Solidifying happens when…

- Melting is a physical process because…

Common misconceptions

Misconception	How to identify	How to overcome
Heating changes a substance into a new substance.	Ask learners what substance ice is made of. What happens to ice when we heat it? Does it change to a new substance?	Give learners a bit of plain chocolate (if they are allowed) to taste. Then melt a square of the same chocolate. (You can do this at the same time as Think like a scientist 2.) How has the chocolate changed? Let one or two learners to taste the melted chocolate. Is it the same substance?

Starter ideas

1 Getting started (5 minutes)

Resources: Learner's Book

Description: Read the questions in the Learner's Book to the learners. Then use the 'Think-pair-share' method to allow learners to think about their answers for a minute or two, then discuss their answer with a partner before sharing their answers with the class.

2 How has it changed? (5 minutes)

Resources: Paper, scissors

Description: Show the class a piece of paper and crumple it up. How has it changed? (Its shape has changed, it is now crumpled.) Ask if it has changed in any other way. Is it still paper? (Yes)

Ask the learners if you can change the paper back to the way it was originally. (Yes, if you smooth it out it or iron it)

Cut the paper into pieces. Can it be changed back? (Yes, if you stick the bits together)

Tell learners that when we change the shape of an object or material the change is called a physical change. The material is still the same, but it has a different shape or form. Explain that they will be learning about different kinds of physical changes in the topic.

If learners say the paper is a different substance when you crumple it or cut it up, you will have identified the misconception.

Main teaching ideas

1 Think like a scientist 1: What happens to ice when it is heated? (20 minutes)

Learning intention: To observe and describe the change in solid ice when it is heated

Resources: Learner's Book. Per group: one ice cube per learner; saucer

Description: In this activity, learners will observe changes over time to ice cubes as they are heated. Read through the instructions in the Learner's Book. The activity draws on learners' prior knowledge and experience by asking them to predict what will happen to ice when it is heated. Then heat the ice and allow learners to observe the change.

Explain the change of state that takes place when we add heat to the ice. The ice gets heat from our hands when we hold an ice cube. Use the term melting. Ask learners if they can think of any other examples of melting.

After the demonstration/investigation, learners answer questions 1–3 in the Learner's Book.

> **Practical guidance:** This is a learner-led activity. Learners should observe that the ice cube starts melting as soon as they hold it. Tell them to put the ice cubes back on the saucer if their hands feel too cold.

You could also compare how fast an ice cube left on the saucer melts with how fast an ice held in a hand melts. This will show that the melting occurs quicker if more heat energy is added to a solid. Ask learners to tell you what they observed. Write the conclusion on the board.

solid phase (ice) ⟶ liquid phase (water)

2 Think like a scientist 2: Compare melting in different solids (20–30 minutes)

Learning intention: To identify factors in a fair test, describe a change of state

Resources: Learner's Book. An ice cube, a square of chocolate, a cube of butter, three saucers and a stopwatch or timer per group; Worksheet 3.3A, 3.3B and 3.3C (optional)

Description: Read through the instructions in the Learner's Book.

Ask learners if they think the solids will all take the same amount of time to melt. Allow learners to do this activity in groups.

> **Practical guidance:** Prepare your items to melt in advance and keep them all in the freezer or fridge so that they don't melt before you start. You could substitute margarine or solid coconut oil for the butter.

Learners should place the solids on separate saucers and place them in a warm place. A group member should check the saucers every 5 minutes and report back when each solid begins to melt. Note that the chocolate may not start to melt if the temperature is lower than 38–40 °C.

As consolidation, learners should answer questions 1 to 6 in the Learner's Book.

As consolidation, learners should answer questions 1 to 6 in the Learner's Book.

Learners can complete Worksheet 3.3A, 3.3B or 3.3C once they've finished the investigation.

> **Differentiation ideas:** More confident learners should be able to answer question 7 in the Learner's Book.

> **Assessment ideas:** Learners can answer these self-assessment questions:

- Can I use the particle model to describe the change of state of a solid when it is heated?

- Can I say if the investigation is a fair test and why or why not?

3   **Digital Classroom Science Investigator video: Do some solids melt more quickly than others? (10–15 minutes)**

Learning intention: To demonstrate how to carry out a fair test and how to measure time

Resources: Digital Classroom Science Investigator video: Do some solids melt more quickly than others?

Description: As an alternative to Think like a scientist 2 you can show the Digital Classroom Science Investigator video 'Do some solids melt more quickly than others?' to guide learners through the investigation. The i button will explain how to the use the Science Investigator video.

Show the video. Pause when indicated to allow learners to answer the questions. Also let them answer the questions at the end of the video.

Answers:

1   Answers depend on learners' predictions.

2   They heated the solids on the same stove, used the same sized solids, used the same pan and started measuring each solid's melting time as soon as the solid was put in the pan.

3   The solid chocolate was heated, this made it melt and become liquid.

4   They could repeat the test a few times to check on their results, weigh the solids instead of measuring size, use three identical pans and stoves and start the melting of each substance at the same time, or any other suitable suggestion.

Plenary ideas

1   **Quick check (5 minutes)**

Description: Let learners stand and quickly say one thing they have learned in the topic before sitting down.

> **Assessment ideas:** Learners' answers should give you a quick overview of how well the class has understood the work covered in the topic.

> **Reflection ideas:** Learners can answer the Reflection questions in the Learner's Book.

2   **Melting and freezing at home (5–10 minutes)**

Description: Hold a class brainstorming session in which learners give examples of how they, or their families, use melting and freezing at home.

Make a mind map of learners' answers on the board.

Measuring time, recording results in a table and drawing a graph in main teaching idea 2 link with measurement, data handling and graphing in Maths.

Homework ideas

1   Learners can draw the bar graphs from Think like a scientist 2 as a homework task.

    You can use the assessment idea for the activity in this guide.

2   Learners could complete the Workbook Focus, Practice and/Challenge sections for Topic 3.3. In the next lesson, discuss answers in class. Allow learners to check their own work.

Topic worksheets

Worksheet 3.3A, 3.3B and 3.3C: Compare melting in different solids

This set of worksheets gives learners the opportunity to practise their skills at reading and drawing graphs.

Less confident learners should attempt Worksheet 3.3A.

Most learners should be able to complete Worksheet 3.3B.

More confident learners can should attempt Worksheet 3.3C.

3.4 Chemical reactions

LEARNING PLAN

Learning objectives	Learning intention	Success criteria
4Cc.03 Know that some substances will react with another substance to produce one or more new substances and this is called a chemical reaction.	• To find out that new substances form in chemical reactions.	• Learners know that new substances form in chemical reactions.
4TWSp.03 Make a prediction describing some possible outcomes of an enquiry.	• To be able to make a prediction for an investigation.	• Learners can make a prediction for an investigation.
4TWSc.07 Use secondary information sources to research an answer to a question.	• To be able to find information to answer a scientific question.	• Learners can find information to answer a scientific question.
4TWSc.08 Collect and record observations and/or measurements in tables and diagrams.	• To be able to make drawings of observations.	• Learners can make drawings of observations.
4TWSa.03 Make a conclusion from results and relate it to the scientific question being investigated.	• To be able to make a conclusion for an investigation.	• Learners can make a conclusion for an investigation.

CONTINUED

Learning objectives	Learning intention	Success criteria
4TWSp.02 Know that there are five main types of scientific enquiry (**research**, fair testing, **observing over time**, identifying and classifying, and pattern seeking).	• To find out that we can obtain results by observing over time. • To be able to answer a scientific question by doing research.	• Learners can understand that we can obtain results by observing over time. • Learners can answer a scientific question by doing research.
4SIC.05 Discuss how the use of science and technology can have positive and negative environmental effects on their local area.	• To discuss how preventing rusting can help the local environment.	• Learners can say how preventing rusting can help the local environment.

LANGUAGE SUPPORT

The main new words for the topic are: chemical reaction, react, rust. Explain each of the terms clearly when you use them for the first time. You can also get learners to say the terms with you a few times.

• **chemical reaction** – when we mix together two substances and they both change to make a new substance. For example, when we mix baking powder and water they both change to make carbon dioxide gas that makes a cake rise

• **react** – this is when a substance changes when it is mixed with another substance. For example,

baking powder reacts with water to make carbon dioxide gas that makes a cake rise

• **rust** – a reddish-brown powder that forms on some metals

If you demonstrate a chemical reaction, as suggested in the teacher notes for the topic, ask learners to explain to one another what they observed. Tell them to use the words 'react' and 'chemical reaction' in their explanation. For example: I saw vinegar and baking soda react together to make a gas. This was a chemical reaction because it made a new substance from the two substances.

Common misconceptions

Misconception	How to identify	How to overcome
Chemical reactions or changes happen when you mix two substances together.	Ask learners what happens if you mix flour and sugar together. Or sand and water? Does a new substance form? Can we separate the substances?	Remind learners that we can separate the substances in some mixtures, e.g. by sieving or filtering. This shows that there is not always a chemical reaction when we mix two substances together.

Starter ideas

1 Getting started (5 minutes)

Resources: Learner's Book

Description: Read the questions in the Learner's Book to the learners. Then use the 'Think-pair-share' method to allow learners to think about their answers for a minute or two, then discuss their answer with a partner before sharing their answers with the class.

Answers to question 4 will help you identify the misconception that chemical reactions or changes happen when you mix two substances together, if learners say that melted chocolate mixed with nuts forms a new substance.

2 Baking a cake (5–10 minutes)

Resources: Picture of a cake, or a real cake

Description: Show learners the cake or the picture of a cake.

Ask:

- Have you ever eaten cake?
- What substances do we use to make the cake?
- Do those substances change or stay the same when mix them together and bake the mixture?

You can then introduce the idea of a chemical reaction – substances in the cake mix such as baking powder and water react and change to form new substances.

Also ask if the cake can be changed back into the substances it is made from. Then explain that in a chemical reaction we cannot change the new substance back into the substances that reacted together.

Main teaching ideas

1 Observe a chemical reaction (15 minutes)

Learning intention: To demonstrate that when two substances react with one other, they both change to form new substances

Resources: per group, jar with a wide mouth, vinegar, bicarbonate of soda (baking soda), teaspoon

Description: This is a learner-led activity in which they will make carbon dioxide gas by mixing together vinegar and bicarbonate of soda (baking soda) as an example of chemical reaction. The activity does not appear in the Learner's Book.

Ask learners to say what they think will happen when you mix the two substances together.

Then let learners do the activity as described below.

At the end, ask learners to describe how the vinegar and bicarbonate of soda changed. What new substance formed? (the gas)

> **Practical guidance:** Learners should work in groups and follow these steps:

- Pour some vinegar into the jar.
- Put a teaspoon of bicarbonate of soda into the jar.
- Observe what happens.

Learners could also make drawings of their observations.

If this is the first time doing this experiment then you can review a video on the internet to show the reaction between the substances.

2 Think like a scientist: Which substances react to form rust? (20–30 minutes, over three days)

Learning intention: To demonstrate that when two substances react with one other, they both change to form new substances

Resources: Learner's Book; three pieces of wire wool, three glass jars and one lid, water, a marking pen

Description: In this activity, learners will investigate which substances react to form rust.

Learners will use the observing changes over time type of scientific enquiry.

Read through the instructions, and ask learners to look at the picture of how to set up the investigation in the Learner's Book.

Learners then follow the instructions and answer the questions.

> **Practical guidance:** This is a learner-led activity.

Learners should work in groups to set up their investigation.

The wire wool in jar 1 must be partly in the liquid but also exposed to air.

Learners should predict what they think will happen in each jar. They will need to record their observations in drawings after two days.

> **Differentiation ideas:** You can help less confident learners to make a conclusion by asking: Which substances do you think reacted to make the wire wool rust?

More confident learners could plan and do an investigation to find out if all metals rust, for example with brass nails, steel nails and iron nails.

> **Assessment ideas:** You can use this checklist to assess learners' investigations:

Were learners able to:	Yes	Needed help
make a prediction?		
record their observations in drawings?		
make a conclusion from their observations which is related to the question investigated?		

3 Activity: How can we prevent rusting? (1–2 hours)

Learning intention: To use secondary sources find information about how to prevent rusting

Resources: Learner's Book, secondary sources such as books and the internet.

Description: Learners will use the research type of scientific enquiry in the activity. Talk about why rusting is a problem. Then explain the task from the Learner's Book.

Ask the learners to think about the results from the Think like a scientist activity. Which substances cause rusting? (water and air) Ask learners how they think rusting can be prevented (don't expose the metal to water and air). You can mention that iron and metals that contain iron, e.g. steel, rust.

Learners should work in pairs. The activity can be done as a homework task if you do not have access to secondary resources in class.

Learners can choose how to present their findings to the class, e.g. a poster or PowerPoint presentation.

> **Assessment ideas:** Learners can assess other pairs' presentations.

Criterion	Yes	Sort of	No
Was the presentation well prepared?			
Did pictures or slides make the presentation more interesting?			
Did the presentation give information about how to stop metals rusting?			
Was the information about how to stop metals rusting easy to understand?			

Plenary ideas

1 I can and I know (5–10 minutes)

Resources: Learners will need paper and pens or pencils

Description: Ask learners to each write two sentences about what they have learnt in the topic. Their sentences should start with either:

I can …

or

I know …

Give learners one or two minutes to write their sentences. Then write or project a list of success criteria onto the board. Learners can compare their sentences with the success criteria to assess if they have grasped the main ideas and skills covered in the topic.

> **Assessment ideas:** This is a self-assessment activity which will help learners to identify areas where they are succeeding or where they need more support.

2 Is it a chemical reaction? (5–10 minutes)

Resources: Chalk, vinegar, beaker or jar; Worksheet 3.4 (optional)

Description: You can demonstrate the activity to the class. Make sure all learners can see what is happening.

Chalk is made from limestone, which is made mostly of calcium carbonate. Vinegar is an acid (acetic acid). The calcium carbonate and vinegar react to form a salt called calcium acetate, water and carbon dioxide gas.

Learners will observe that the chalk disappears and bubbles of gas form.

Put a piece of chalk into the beaker or jar. Pour some vinegar over the chalk.

Get learners to observe what happens. Ask learners to work in pairs to say if that have observed a chemical reaction and why or why not.

(It is a chemical reaction because:

Two substances react (chalk and vinegar)

Both the substances change

A new substance forms.)

Alternatively, you use Worksheet 3.4 with learners. The Help sheet can be given to less confident learners and the Stretch sheet can be used to challenge more confident learners.

> **Reflection ideas:** Learners can answer the Reflection question in the Learner's Book.

CROSS-CURRICULAR LINKS

The reading and writing activities in main teaching idea 3 can be linked to English.

Homework ideas

1   Learners could complete the Activity: How can we prevent rusting? Learners can assess other pairs' presentations using the checklist in the teacher notes on the activity.

2   Learners could complete the Workbook Focus, Practice and Challenge sections for Topic 3.4. In the next lesson, discuss the answers in class. Allow learners to check their own work.

Topic worksheets

Worksheet 3.4: Observe chemical reactions

This practical worksheet provides more opportunity for observation of chemical reactions. Part 1 is a teacher demonstration. Part 2 is learner-led.

In Part 1, learners will observe and identify the physical changes and chemical changes that take place when a candle burns. In Part 2, learners will create their own chemical reaction using vinegar and sodium bicarbonate.

Most learners should be able to answer questions 1–3 in Parts 1 and 2. There is a Help sheet for learners who need more support in identifying chemical changes.

More confident learners should be able answer questions 4 and 5 on the Stretch sheet for Parts 1 and 2. They may need to do some research for Part 2.

PROJECT: FROZEN FOODS

LEARNING OBJECTIVES

4SIC.01 Describe how science is used in their local area.

Refer to the Learner's Book. Discuss the different parts of the project with the class before they begin. You may choose to ask more confident and proficient learners to complete all three parts. Other learners could complete Parts 1 and 3 only, if you choose.

Part 1

Learners should work in pairs to collect their information. They may have to be accompanied by an older sibling or relative.

It may be better to speak to the person in their own language if they do not speak English. Learners can then translate the information into English. Assist them with this if needed.

Part 2

In this part of the project, learners can work in groups of 4–5 to plan and carry out an investigation to answer a question about the freezing times of different foods. They can ask their own question to investigate, or choose one of the suggested questions.

Learners should record their measurements in a table and present their results in a graph.

Their conclusion should be related to the question they investigated.

Part 3

Each pair of learners should produce a presentation for assessment. Their presentations should include the use of visual materials such as pictures, graphs and drawings. For example, they can choose to make a poster or PowerPoint slides.

Learners should present their findings shows to the class. Remind them to speak clearly and to look at their audience from time to time (make eye contact).

Assessment

You could use this rubric to assess learners' projects.

SIC LOs	Beginning	Developing	Mastering
Obtain information about frozen foods from local people.	Obtains no or very little usable information about frozen foods from local people.	Obtains adequate information about frozen foods from local people.	Obtains detailed, useful information about frozen foods from local people.
TWS LOs			
Ask a scientific question to investigate.	Struggles to ask a question to investigate, or asks a question that is not testable.	With guidance, asks a testable question, or asks a question that may not be testable.	Asks a testable question.

SIC LOs	Beginning	Developing	Mastering
TWS LOs			
Identify variables that need to be taken into account when fair testing.	Identifies one or two variables that need to be taken into account in planning a fair test.	Identifies most variables that need to be taken into account in planning a fair test.	Identifies all variables that need to be taken into account in planning a fair test.
Choose equipment from a suggested selection and use it appropriately.	Struggles to choose equipment from a suggested selection and use it appropriately.	Needs help choosing equipment from a suggested selection and uses it appropriately.	Chooses suitable equipment from a suggested selection and uses it appropriately.
Measure and record freezing time of foods in minutes and hours.	Unable to record freezing time of foods in minutes and hours.	With assistance, can record freezing time of foods in minutes and hours.	Accurately records freezing time of foods in minutes and hours.
Record measurements in a table.	Unable to correctly record measurements in a table.	Needs help to correctly record measurements in a table.	Can correctly record measurements in a table.
Present results in a graph.	Struggles to draw any graph of the results.	With assitance, draws a suitable graph of the results.	Draws a suitable graph of the results.
Make a conclusion from results and relate it to the scientific question investigated.	Unable to make a conclusion, or makes a conclusion not related to results and the scientific question investigated.	With asssistance, makes a suitable conclusion from results and relates it to the scientific question investigated.	Makes a suitable conclusion from results and relates it to the scientific question investigated.
Presentation			
Presentation content.	Poorly prepared, with little correct or relvant information presented.	Adequately prepared, information correct and relevant.	Well-prepared, information detailed, correct and relevant.
Use of slides, pictures or other visual material.	No or very little use of suitable slides, pictures or other visual material.	Some use of suitable slides, pictures or other visual material.	Very good use of suitable slides, pictures or other visual material.

> 4 Earth and its habitats

Unit plan

Topic	Approximate number of learning hours	Outline of learning content	Resources
4.1 The structure of the Earth	1.5	• Describe a model of the structure of the Earth	**Learner's Book:** Activity: Summarise the structure of the Earth Think like a scientist: Use a model to explain the structure of the Earth **Workbook:** Topic 4.1 ⬇ Worksheet 4.1 **Digital Classroom:** Activity – The structure of the Earth
4.2 Volcanoes	2	• Identify volcanoes from pictures and diagrams and location on world map	**Learner's Book:** Activity 1: Describe the features of a volcano Think like a scientist: Draw a diagram of a volcano Activity 2: Describe where volcanoes erupt Activity 3: What have I learnt about volcanoes? **Workbook:** Topic 4.2 **Digital Classroom:** Video – Volcanoes
4.3 Earthquakes	2	• Find out that earthquakes and tsunamis result from sudden movements of the Earth's crust	**Learner's Book:** Activity 1: Find information about earthquakes Activity 2: Case study: an earthquake in Chile **Workbook:** Topic 4.3 **Digital Classroom:** Video – Earthquakes
4.4 Different habitats	3, including bird watching and feedback	• See how different animals are suited to their habitat and apply this to observing birds	**Learner's Book:** Activity 1: How birds are suited to different habitats Activity 2: How are tigers suited to their habitat? Think like a scientist: Bird watching **Workbook:** Topic 4.4 ⬇ Worksheet 4.4A, 4.4B and 4.4C **Digital Classroom:** Video – Birds in different habitats

Across unit resources

Learner's Book:

Project: How people use science

Check your progress quiz

Teacher's Resource:

⬇ Language worksheets 1 & 2

⬇ End-of-unit test

⬇ Diagnostic check

⬇ Mid-point test

⬇ End-of-year test

Digital Classroom: End-of-unit quiz

BACKGROUND KNOWLEDGE

Learning about the Earth's structure is part of a branch of science called Geology. Many learners are fascinated by this because it is something they can relate to because Geology is all around us. The area they live in may have hills, valleys, rivers, different rocks and quite possibly volcanoes and earthquakes. As their teacher you can help them with local examples.

In Stage 4 we begin with the structure of the Earth, which in some ways is difficult because it is an area where scientists have limited evidence! Nobody has ever dug further than the Earth's crust. Scientists can be fairly sure of what the mantle consists of because material from the mantle comes to the surface as volcanoes. Ideas about the composition of the core are more

complicated and involve the Earth's magnetic field.

In this unit we have simplified the causes of volcanoes and earthquakes to be due to 'Earth movements'. Learners will revisit this in Stage 7 when they will learn that the Earth's crust actually consists of tectonic plates and it is along the plate boundaries that we find earthquake and volcanic activity.

Some learners may want to know how old the Earth is. Our planet and the rest of the solar system was formed 4600 million years ago – a very difficult time frame for us to understand. It may help to compare this timeframe with when dinosaurs died out on Earth – this was 65 million years ago. Even soil can take hundreds of years to form.

TEACHING SKILLS FOCUS

Visual literacy – using photographs as a teaching tool

In this unit we make use of photographs quite often. Photographs and diagrams are part of visual literacy – learning from visual stimuli such as photographs and diagrams rather than words. For many learners this is a very effective way of

learning, especially if their language skills are less developed.

Photographs are a good teaching tool because they show examples of the 'real thing'. Learners can take their own photographs to illustrate projects. They can do this in the bird watching activity in topic 4.4 and in the project.

CONTINUED

You can help your learners to find information from a photograph by asking questions like these:

- What is the main feature of the photograph?

- What clues do I have to show me where the photograph was taken? E.g. outside or inside, countryside or city.

- What clues do I have about the landscape? For example, mountains, sea, river.

- Are there animals in the photograph? Can we identify them?

- What clues are there about the climate? Does it look hot, cold, dry or wet?

- Are there people in the photograph? What are they doing?

- How are the people dressed – can we guess where they come from?

When you look at photographs of earthquake damage in the Learner's Book, learners can identify damage that the earthquake has caused. You can also ask questions such as 'How would you feel if your home was destroyed by an earthquake?' or 'How do people manage to bring help if roads and bridges collapse?'

A video or slide show of a volcanic eruption and earthquake damage will make a big impression on learners and make them keen to know how these events happen.

You can get well-illustrated books from the library to show learners photographs of volcanoes, earthquakes and different habitats. Ask suitable questions such as the ones in the above list to train the learners to get as much information as they can.

4.1 The structure of the Earth

LEARNING PLAN

Learning objectives	Learning intention	Success criteria
4ESp.01 Describe the model of the structure of the Earth which includes a core, a mantle and a crust.	• To be able to describe a model of the structure of the Earth.	• Learners can use a model to describe the internal structure of the Earth.
4TWSm.01 Know that models are not fully representative of a real-world situation and/or scientific idea.	• To discuss how a model can never be a true copy of the real thing.	• Learners can understand that a model can never be a true copy of the real thing.
4TWSm.02 Use models to show relationships, quantities or scale.	• To be able to use models to show relationships, quantities or scale.	• Learners can use a model to name and describe the layers of the interior of the Earth.

LANGUAGE SUPPORT

- **core** – the centre of the Earth. 'Core' is a commonly used word in English that always means 'at the centre of'. For example, the core of an apple is at the centre of the apple, the core ideas are the ideas most central to the topic

- **crust** – the outer layer of the Earth. Note that 'crust' is also used in English to describe the hard outer layer of bread

- **external structure** – materials that make up the surface of the Earth. 'External' means 'outside', so we are referring to materials on the surface of the Earth that we can see

- **internal structure** – materials that make up the inside of the Earth. 'Internal' means 'inside' so we are referring to materials inside the Earth that we can't see

- **magma** – melted rocks

- **mantle** – the layer of the Earth below the crust which consists of magma

Some learners may have difficulty understanding some of the text about the crust, the mantle and the core, which is why they can't answer some of the questions. Ask them which words or sentences they do not understand and simplify the text for them until they know what it means. Here are some possible words that they may have difficulty with:

- **outer and inner** – these adjectives mean the object nearest to the outside and the object nearest to the inside, e.g. the inner core and the outer core.

- **'thicker than'** and **'thinner than'**, **'thinnest'** and **'thickest'** are comparative forms of the adjectives thick and thin. For example, in this topic:
  - The crust is **thinner than** the other layers. The crust is the **thinnest** layer.
  - The mantle is **thicker than** the crust and the core. The mantle is the **thickest** layer.

- Hotter than, colder than, hottest and coldest. For example, in this topic:
  - The mantle is **hotter than** the crust. The inner core is the **hottest** layer.

Common misconceptions

Misconception	How to identify	How to overcome
The whole of the Earth is formed of solid rocks like the surface.	Ask learners to tell you what is below the rocks and sea on the satellite photograph on the opening page of this topic.	Complete the Learner's Book Activity: Summarise the structure of the Earth to correct misunderstandings. Learners will see that there are different materials in the mantle, the inner core and outer core.

Starter ideas

1 Getting started (5–10 minutes)

Resources: Learner's Book; satellite photograph and questions

Description: Tell learners to look at the satellite photograph and tell you what they see (they should say rocks and sea). When you ask them what they think might be underneath the surface of the Earth they might say more rocks. This is a misconception that you will try to overcome during the lesson as you teach them about the internal layers of the Earth.

Take note of learners' answers to question 3 in the Learner's Book (What do you think might be underneath the surface?). Complete the Learner's Book Activity: Summarise the structure of the Earth to overcome this misconception.

2 What is this? (5 minutes)

Resources: A chunk of lava from a volcano or piece of pumice stone

Description: Obtain a sample (this will work well in volcanic areas especially) and show it to learners. Ask them:

- What is this? (If learners do not know, tell them that it has come from a volcano.)
- Where does it come from? (Deep beneath the surface of the Earth)
- Was it always solid? (No, it was liquid and it came out of a volcano and then cooled down to form this rock.)

Take note of learners' answers to question 3 in the Learner's Book (What do you think might be underneath the surface?). This demonstration will show learners that there is liquid material below the surface of the Earth.

Main teaching ideas

1 Activity: Summarise the structure of the Earth (10 minutes)

Learning intention: To consolidate information about internal structure of Earth

Resources: Learner's Book, Digital Classroom activity: the structure of the Earth (optional)

Description: Ask learners to copy and complete the table in the Learner's Book. Learners use information in the text and on the diagram to complete the table. This is a good exercise in transferring information from one form to another. It is not necessary for learners to remember all the distances and temperatures. At this age learners like looking at numbers and will be amazed, for example, that the crust is so thin compared to the other layers. You can give local examples of the distances such as it being 5 km or 70 km or 3000 km to a certain place. And they can compare the temperatures with water boiling at 100°C.

> **Digital Classroom:** If you have access to the Digital Classroom component, use the activity 'The structure of the Earth' to consolidate learner's knowledge of the layers which make up the Earth. The i button will explain how to use the activity.

> **Differentiation ideas:** This is an activity all learners should be able to do. If they struggle it could be because they do not understand some of the text. Ask which words or sentences they do not understand and help them by simplifying the text further.

> **Assessment ideas:** Go through answers in class.

2 Think like a scientist: Use a model to explain the structure of the Earth (15 minutes)

Learning intention: Describe a model of the structure of the Earth and discuss how a model can never be a true copy of the real thing.

Resources: Learner's Book; a piece of fruit, a knife to cut fruit, a board to cut on.

Bring to class a piece of round-shaped fruit with a stone and a thin skin – like a peach, a plum or litchi. Cut the fruit in half like the diagram in the Learner's Book.

Description: Show the cut fruit to learners and discuss answers to Learner's Book questions 1, 2 and 3 in class. Write learners' answers on the board.

Learners can work in pairs to answer questions 4 and 5 and then report back. Question 4 is an example of 4SIC.01 Describe how scientific knowledge and understanding changes over time through the use of evidence gained by enquiry.

> **Differentiation ideas:** Learners need to read and understand the text about the core to answer question 4. Question 5 is an extension question that requires lateral thinking.

3 Workbook 4.1: The structure of the Earth (10–15 minutes each)

Learning intention: Describe a model of the structure of the Earth and discuss how a model can never be a true copy of the real thing.

Resources: Workbook 4.1

Description: Learners should follow the instructions in the Workbook and write or draw their answers in the spaces provided.

> **Differentiation ideas:** All learners should be able to do the Focus exercise, although there may be some vocabulary they are not familiar with, such as use of comparative terms such as thicker than, thinner than, hotter than, cooler than.

All learners should also be able to do the Practice exercise.

The Challenge exercise is more difficult. Learners need to be able to read and understand the text to answer the questions.

Plenary ideas

1 Self-assessment (5 minutes)

Resources: Learner's Book

Description: Ask learners to explain the internal structure of the Earth to a younger person such as a brother or sister. They should use a model such as a round fruit.

2 Worksheet 4.1: Plan and make your own model (10 minutes for planning at end of lesson)

Resources: Worksheet 4.1

Description: Learners can choose a friend to work with and plan their model for the worksheet in class at the end of the lesson and finish for homework.

CROSS-CURRICULAR LINKS

Main teaching idea 1 links with energy and the particle model in Unit 3, as well as measurement of temperature in degrees in Maths.

Main teaching idea 2 links with matter and the particle model in Unit 3.

Main teaching idea 3 links with English – use of comparative terms such as thicker than, thinner than, hotter than, cooler than.

Most activities also link with Geography.

Homework ideas

1 Workbook 4.1 exercises (go through answers in class and learners can correct own work).

2 Ask learners to present their ideas for their model in Worksheet 4.1. They may even make a model to bring to class.

Topic worksheets

Worksheet 4.1: Plan and make your own model

This worksheet is suitable for all learners. Learners have to plan how they would make a model of the internal structure of the Earth. Encourage them to actually make the model and bring it to class.

4.2 Volcanoes

LEARNING PLAN

Learning objectives	Learning intention	Success criteria
4ESp.02 Describe common features of volcanoes and know they are found at breaks in the Earth's crust.	• To be able to identify features of volcanoes from pictures and diagrams.	• Learners can describe common features of volcanoes. • Learners can use a model to help them understand how a volcano forms.
4TWSm.02 Use models to show relationships, quantities or scale.	• To be able to use a map to describe where volcanoes occur at breaks in the Earth's crust.	• Learners can use a map to describe where volcanoes occur at breaks in the Earth's crust.
4TWSm.03 Draw a diagram to represent a real-world situation and/or scientific idea.	• To be able to draw a diagram to represent a real volcano.	• Learners can draw a diagram to represent a real volcano.

LANGUAGE SUPPORT

Learners will use the following words in the topic:

- **ash** – burnt material. For example, the grey powdery material left when wood has burnt

- **composite volcano** – a volcano that erupts lava and ash which builds up into a cone-shaped mountain. 'Composite' means being made up of more than one type of material

- **crater** – a large hole at the top of a volcano where material erupts

- **erupt** – a verb which means to shoot out suddenly. For example, if you boil milk in a saucepan and do not watch it, the milk can erupt out of the pan and on to the stove

- **lava** – magma that reaches the surface of the Earth

- **plateau** – a flat uplifted area of rock. For example, most of India and Africa consists of a plateau

- **risk** – the possibility of something happening. For example, if you climb a tree, there's a risk you might fall

- **secondary cone** – a small volcano that erupts on the side of the main volcano

- **vent** – a hole. For example, buildings have vents built into them to allow air in. The vents are grids with holes in

Learners will also benefit from understanding the following words and phrases:

- **eruption** – this is the noun. When a volcano erupts we say there has been a volcanic eruption.

- **having a high risk of volcanic eruption** – a phrase meaning it is very likely that a volcano will erupt.

- **having a low risk of volcanic eruption** – a phrase meaning there is very little chance that a volcano will erupt.

Common misconceptions

Misconception	How to identify	How to overcome
All volcanoes are cone-shaped mountains.	Ask learners to tell you what a volcano looks like.	Show learners the photograph of the Hawaii volcanoes in the Learner's Book, which shows very runny lava flowing outwards, to demonstrate that it is making a raised flat surface rather than a cone-shaped mountain.

Starter ideas

1 Watch a volcanic eruption (5–10 minutes)

Resources: Digital Classroom video: Volcanoes (optional). Or search for 'recent volcanic eruption' on the internet and you will find a selection of short videos.

> **Digital Classroom:** If you have access to the Digital Classroom component, use the video 'Volcanoes' to show learners a volcanic eruption. The i button will explain how to use the video.

Alternatively, show a video clip you've found on the internet. Ask learners the following questions:

- What did the video show? (A volcanic eruption/ volcano)

- What is coming out of the volcano? (What the video shows – could be black smoke, lava, ash, rocks)

- Where do you think this material comes from? (The layer of the Earth below the crust – the mantle)

2 Hot stuff (5 minutes)

Resources: Large photographs of volcanic eruptions. Find one photograph of a cone-shaped composite volcano and another of a Hawaiian 'flat' volcano (use an internet search or a library).

Description: Show learners photographs of different types of volcanic eruptions. Ask the following questions:

- What is coming out of the volcano? (Depending on photographs – try to find some showing lava, others smoke, rocks, ash)

- Does this material make a mountain or a flat surface? (It can do either depending on how runny the lava is and whether there are other types of material such as ash)

- What does the material form when it has cooled down? (Rock)

Main teaching ideas

1 Questions about photographs of volcanoes (5–10 minutes)

Learning intention: These questions will guide learners to be able to identify volcanoes from photographs.

Resources: Photographs and the diagram in the Learner's Book; any other appropriate photographs that you can find (in books, newspapers or magazines, or on the internet).

Description: Show learners the volcano photo and diagram in the Learner's Book, and ask the questions in class. For questions 1 and 2 the learners must point to the features on the photograph. The red material is the lava and the black material is lava that has hardened into rock. For question 3 it will help if you have some extra photographs. Describe the volcano in the diagram and photograph as shaped like a cone-shaped mountain with smooth sides. However, some volcanoes are flat. It depends on how runny the lava is and whether there are layers of ash.

Learners can consolidate by doing **Activity 1: Describe the features of a volcano**, in class. This will help learners to compare what they can see on a diagram with what they can see in a photograph. They can work in pairs or on their own. When they have finished go through the answers in class. Ask for suggestions and collect answers from different learners.

2 Think like a scientist: Draw a diagram of a volcano (10–15minutes)

Learning intention: Draw a diagram to represent a real-world situation – in this case, a volcano.

Resources: Diagram and photograph in Learner's Book.

Description: Show learners the photograph of the volcano next to the diagram in the Learner's Book and tell them to draw a diagram of that photograph. Learners must be careful <u>not</u> to copy the diagram of the volcano in the Learner's Book. Their task is to make a diagram of the volcano in the photograph next to the diagram. They should try to copy the shape of the volcano in the photograph and then add in the interior structure. (This will be the same as on the diagram in the Learner's Book, except they should <u>not</u> put in the secondary cone or side vent because there is no secondary cone on the photograph.) Tell learners to use a soft pencil and use an eraser when necessary. They can colour their diagram when you have checked the outlines. Walk around the class and check that learners are not just copying the diagram in the Learner's Book.

> **Differentiation ideas:** Some learners will be better than others at this skill. Encourage those who are not natural artists! As long as the diagram shows the correct parts of the volcano and is neatly labelled it will be fine. Drawing diagrams is an important skill in Science.

> **Assessment ideas:** Encourage learners to answer the Self-assessment questions in the Learner's Book after they have drawn their diagrams.

3 Activity 2: Describe where volcanoes erupt (10–15 minutes)

Learning intention: To describe where volcanoes erupt at breaks in the Earth's crust.

Learners must be able to point out on a world map where there are breaks in the Earth's crust and volcanoes are likely to occur.

Resources: A map of the distribution of volcanoes in the Learner's Book and Workbook, plus a globe if you have one.

Description: If you have a globe, show learners where your country is on the globe. Then show them the Pacific Ocean. Then move on to the 'flat map' in the Learner's Book. Help them to name the countries. Then focus on where the volcanoes are.

Answer the questions in the Learner's Book in class.

For question 5 find Indonesia and the Philippines on the map.

⟩ **Differentiation ideas:** Learners who have used maps before will be at an advantage. They can help others find the countries on the map and the globe.

4 Positive and negative effects of volcanoes – extension activity (10 minutes)

Learning intention: To show learners that volcanoes can have both negative and positive effects for people living close to them. This is an example of 4SIC.05 Discuss how use of science and technology can have positive and negative environment effects on local area.

Resources: Annotated drawing of a volcano and surrounding area in the Learner's Book.

Description: First ask learners what they think are the negative effects of living next to a volcano. From the lesson so far, they should be able to tell you the dangers of lava and ash and landslides. Ask them why they think so many people do live on the slopes of volcanoes. If possible project the drawing on to a screen. Show learners the positive effects. Ask learners if they know people who live close to a volcano and if so what do these people do for a living.

Plenary ideas

1 Activity 3: What have I learnt about volcanoes? (10 minutes)

Resources: Learner's Book

Description: Read the text about the two volcanoes aloud to the class. Find the island of Sicily and the Democratic Republic of Congo on the world map or globe. Note that Sicily is in an area where volcanoes are active. This is because chunks of the Earth's crust are moving past each other. Goma in DRC is not far from the Great African Rift Valley, which is also an area where the Earth's crust is moving.

Learners should answer the questions in their notebooks.

⟩ **Assessment ideas:** When learners have finished writing their answers, go through answers in class so that they can check their work.

2 Workbook 4.2: Focus exercise (5–10 minutes)

Resources: Workbook 4.2

Description: Learners fill in their answers in the Workbook.

CROSS-CURRICULAR LINKS

Main teaching idea 1 links with English – reading and writing skills.

Main teaching idea 3 links with Geography or Social Sciences (map skills) or Life Skills.

Homework ideas

The Focus, Practice and Challenge exercises in the Workbook. For the Practice exercise you could project the map (see answers) on the board so that learners could mark their own work.

4.3 Earthquakes

LEARNING PLAN

Learning objectives	Learning intention	Success criteria
4ESp.03 Know that the Earth's crust moves and when parts move suddenly this is called an earthquake.	• To find out that sudden movements of the Earth's crust can result in earthquakes. • To understand how an earthquake can result in a tsunami.	• Learners can understand that an earthquake happens when there are sudden movements of rock in the Earth's crust. • Learners can describe how a tsunami can result from an earthquake.
4TWSm.02 Use models to show relationships, quantities or scale.	• To be able to use a model to understand how an earthquake happens.	• Learners can use a model to understand how an earthquake can happen. • Learners can recognise earthquake damage on photographs.

LANGUAGE SUPPORT

- **coastal area** – a low lying area along the border between land and sea. The coastline is the outline of the border between the land and the sea as you see it on a map
- **earthquake** – a shaking of the Earth
- **epicentre** – the point on the surface of the Earth immediately above the focus. The epicentre is where the most damage occurs
- **focus** – the point in the crust under the Earth's surface where the earthquake starts. We also use the word 'focus' in English to mean the central point. For example, the focus of the lesson was earthquakes
- **landslide** – a mass of rocks and soil that slides down a slope. The vibrations from the earthquake cause these to happen
- **transfers** – changes into. For example, the energy of an earthquake transfers to waves. Learners have come across this word in the unit on Energy (Unit 2.2)

- **tsunami** – a huge wave which happens when an earthquake starts under the sea
- **wave** – a way in which energy travels, for example earthquakes travel through the Earth's crust in waves. A good way to show something similar to one type of earthquake wave is to drop a stone in water – the waves you get spreading outwards will be similar to an earthquake wave (although of course an earthquake wave is much bigger). Demonstrate this in class if you can

In the case study about the earthquake in Chile there are some words and phrases learners may not understand:

- **just off the coast** – very close to the coast in the sea
- **tremors** – weaker shakes
- **coastal towns** – towns built along the coastline

CONTINUED

- **blackout** – a power outage caused by power lines being destroyed as a result of the earthquake
- **people went missing** – people disappeared. They could have been buried by the fallen buildings or landslides or just could not

contact their relatives because they had no communications

- **lost their homes** – they lost their homes because their homes were destroyed by the earthquake

Common misconceptions

Misconception	How to identify	How to overcome
Earthquakes and tsunamis are two completely different events.	Ask learners how they think the tsunami in the picture in Workbook happened.	In the section on tsunamis in the Learner's Book, it is explained that a tsunami is a huge wave which results from an earthquake or a volcanic eruption under the sea.

Starter ideas

1 Watch a video of an earthquake (5–10 minutes)

Resources: Digital Classroom video: Earthquakes (optional), or you can search the internet for 'recent earthquakes' to find a selection of short videos.

> **Digital Classroom:** If you have access to the Digital Classroom component, show the video 'Earthquakes' to lead a class discussion on earthquakes. The i button will explain how to use the video.

Alternatively, show a video clip that you have found on the internet.

Ask learners:

- What did the video show? (Shaking, an earthquake)
- What damage can you see?
- What do you think could cause an earthquake? (Think back to how volcanoes happen – earthquakes also occur due to breaks in the crust)

2 Getting started (5 minutes)

Resources: Learner's Book

Description: Go through the instructions in the Learner's Book with learners. The idea is to demonstrate a transfer of energy so that learners are better able to understand that earthquakes transfer

earth movements to waves. Ask learners question 1 (answer: rubbing) and question 2 (answer: heat).

Main teaching ideas

1 Activity 1: Find information about earthquakes (10 minutes)

Learning intention: To find out that sudden movements of the Earth's crust can result in earthquakes.

Resources: Diagram of an earthquake in the Earth's crust in the Learner's Book; photographs of earthquake damage in the Learner's Book; world map to show Pacific Ring of Fire (from previous topic in the Learner's Book). Can be supplemented with more photographs of different earthquake damage to use for extension questions (see below).

Description: Display the Learner's Book photographs of the earthquakes to the class on a screen. Ask learners questions 1, 3 and 4 from the Learner's Book and discuss the answers.

Ask learners question 2 and refer them to the diagram in the Learner's Book to help them with the answer.

For question 5, display the world map from the previous topic on the screen to show learners where Nepal and Mexico are. Mexico is on the Pacific Ring of Fire. Nepal is in the Himalaya mountains, which is another part of the world where rock sections are crashing past each other inside the Earth's crust. So, the location of Nepal and Mexico means that they are highly at risk of having earthquakes as well as volcanoes.

> **Differentiation ideas:** You can support learners as they find the answers to the questions. For example, when describing the damage on a photograph you can ask guiding questions such as 'What happened to the buildings?' 'Why do you think they fell over?' When using the map revise the Pacific Ring of Fire. Ask learners again what it is. Explain that the same breaks in the rock that form volcanoes can also be responsible for earthquakes.

As an extension question you could find photographs of different types of earthquake damage (such as landslides, flooding, fallen electricity pylons) and ask learners to identify the damage and how it occurred.

2 Questions about earthquakes and tsunamis (5 minutes)

Learning intention: Understand that an earthquake happens when there are sudden movements of rock in the Earth's crust.

This activity will correct the misconception that tsunamis and earthquakes are not related events.

Learners should apply what they have found out about tsunamis to be able to answer the question.

Resources: Photograph in the Learner's Book. You could also show them other photographs of tsunamis you have found.

Description: Show learners the photograph of the boat on top of the building in the Learner's Book. Ask learners question 4. They should be amazed by the height at which the boat came in on the wave.

In questions 1–3, learners must relate what they see with what they know about how a tsunami starts (in the text above the Learner's Book questions).

> **Differentiation ideas:** Some learners will take longer than others to unfold the sequence of events leading up to what is shown on the photograph.

3 Activity 2: Case study: an earthquake in Chile (30 minutes)

Learning intention: Use a real example of an earthquake to find out that sudden movements of the Earth's crust can result in earthquakes.

Resources: Case study with a map and photographs in the Learner's Book.

Description: Project the photographs and map from the case study on the board and read the case study in class. Ask learners what some of the words mean; for example, tremors (shakes) and blackout (no electricity). Show learners where Peru is on the map. Look at a globe or the world map to show them where California and Japan are so that they realise how far away from Chile the effects of the tsunami were felt.

> **Differentiation ideas:** The questions become more difficult towards the end so some learners may need help at this stage.

> **Assessment ideas:** Discuss the answers in class. Learners can check their own work.

Plenary ideas

1 Workbook 4.3: Focus exercise (5–10 minutes)

Resources: Workbook 4.3

Description: This exercise offers a good opportunity for learners to consolidate what they have learnt about Earthquakes in the unit. Learners can read the questions and fill in their answers.

> **Assessment ideas:** Learners can swap workbooks with a partner and mark each other's work.

2 Self-assessment (5 minutes)

Resources: Learner's Book

Description: This topic and the previous one have involved getting information from photographs and maps. Use the self-assessment questions in the Learner's Book to give an indication of how learners feel they are coping with this skill.

> **Assessment ideas:** Learners answer the self-assessment questions.

- Focus exercise – this is good for consolidation.
- Practice exercise – this provides practice in using a photograph to find out about earthquakes.
- Challenge exercise – a case study which demands good reading and comprehension skills and has interesting information about how to reduce damage from earthquakes.

You can take in learners' workbooks and mark them or you can set aside time at the beginning of the next lesson to go through answers in class.

> **CROSS-CURRICULAR LINKS**
>
> Main teaching ideas 1–3 link with energy transfers in Unit 2, as well as Geography or Social Sciences.

Homework ideas

Learners could do the Workbook Focus, Practice and Challenge sections for topic 4.3.

4.4 Different habitats

LEARNING PLAN

Learning objectives	Learning intention	Success criteria
4Be.01 Know that different animals are found in, and suited to, different habitats.	• To see how different animals are suited to their habitat. • To observe birds and how they are suited to the habitat in which they are found.	• Learners can look at examples of how different animals are suited to their habitat. • Learners can see how birds with different beaks eat different food and are suited to different habitats.
4Be.02 Know plants and animals can survive in environments other than their habitats.	• To know that plants and animals can survive in environments other than their habitats.	• Learners realise that plants and animals can survive in places that are not their normal habitat.
4TWSc.01 Use observations and tests to sort, group and classify objects.	• To be able to use observation to classify birds.	• Learners can watch birds eating and classify them according to the shape of their beak.
4TWSc.08 Collect and record observations and/or measurements in tables and diagrams. **4TWSc.04** Describe how repeated measurements and/or observations can give more reliable data.	• To be able to collect and record observations in tables and diagrams. • To see how repeating observations gives more reliable data.	• Learners can record observations in tables and drawings. • Learners can observe birds at different times and find out that this gives them more reliable data.
4TSWa.04 Present and interpret results using tables, bar charts and dot plots.	• To be able to present and interpret results on a dot plot.	• Learners can present and interpret their bird observations on a dot plot.

LANGUAGE SUPPORT

- **beak** – the part of a bird used to catch and hold food

- **crack open** – to break something open.

- **fins** – small flat organs on a fish's body which help it to swim

- **gills** – an organ that fish have to allow them to breathe

- **strain** – to separate solids from the liquid they are in. For example, you use a strainer in the kitchen to separate solid foods from a liquid

Adjectives are used a lot in this topic. For example, we describe a bird's beak with many different adjectives: small, large, long, short, pointed, hooked, sharp, thin and thick.

You could help learners to remember these by making cards with the adjectives on and hold them up when you are describing a photograph, for example.

When you read the 'How are tigers suited to their habitat?' story you may need to explain some of the following words and phrases:

- **blend in well** – mingle with or merge into so that it's difficult to see it

- **sunlight filtering through from the tops of the tree to the forest floor** – the tops of the trees block parts of the sunbeams, causing a pattern of light and shade on the forest floor which is like the tiger's stripes

- **moving around** – moving from place to place

Common misconceptions

Misconception	How to identify	How to overcome
Animals have always been the same as we see them today.	When you are looking at pictures of animals or birds throughout this topic (for example, the different birds in this topic, the polar bear and giraffe in the Workbook and the orangutan in the Worksheets) you can ask the question: Has this animal always looked like this? For example, has the giraffe always had a long neck?	Tell learners that animals do change but over a long period of time (hundreds of thousands of years) so that they can live in a certain habitat. For example, the polar bear and the brown bear are closely related, but the polar bear developed white fur to suit its habitat. Learners do not need to know about this at Stage 4 and they will learn about adaptations, evolution and inheritance later on, but it is a good idea to prepare them for what is to come.

Starter ideas

1 Getting started (5–10 minutes)

Resources: Learner's Book.

Description: Show learners the photographs of two contrasting habitats and describe them. Discuss questions 1 and 2. In question 2 they think about which habitat would have more animals. The tropical forest is likely to have more animals because there is more food available. However, there are many small animals and insects and birds that manage to survive in semi-desert habitats.

2 How is this animal suited to its habitat? (5–10 minutes)

Resources: A picture or pictures of an animal in its natural habitat (not a pet). For example, a lion.

Description: Show learners the photographs of animals and ask them:

- What is this animal? (E.g. a lion)

- What habitat does it live in? (E.g. African grasslands, hot and dry)

- What does it eat? (E.g. other animals)

- How can it eat these? (E.g. huge teeth for eating smaller animals and claws for catching animals)

- How can it hide so that its prey doesn't know it is hunting? (E.g. same colour as its habitat, quiet because of soft pads on feet, runs very fast)

Main teaching ideas

1 Activity 1: How birds are suited to different habitats (10 minutes)

Learning intention: See how different animals are suited to their habitat.

Know that plants and animals can survive in environments other than their habitats.

Resources: Learner's Book

Description: Ask learners to read through the opening pages of the Learner's Book and to copy and complete the table.

Discuss in class the answers to questions 2 and 3.

Ask question 2 and see what answers the learners suggest. Often a park or garden has a variety of trees and plants that you do not find in a natural habitat. This is one reason why different birds can survive there. Also, people give birds food that they do not find in their habitat which helps them to survive, for example, during months of the year when their normal food is not available. Try to think of examples in your area.

Ask question 3 and see what answers the learners suggest. Seagulls catch and eat fish but they are also are scavengers (they live off dead meat or fish). This means they can follow a fishing boat into the harbour and eat fish heads that are thrown in the water or they fly inland and eat food on rubbish dumps in order to survive.

2 Think like a scientist: Bird watching (30–60 minutes)

Learning intention: Observe birds and how they are suited to the habitat in which they are found.

Resources: Learner's Book; birds in their natural habitat, such as a garden, a park, farmland, riverside, seashore; notebook and pencil (one per learner); Digital Classroom video: Birds in different habitats (optional). Learners can record their observations by copying and completing a table like the one below, OR they can design their own observation sheet, as long as it contains the same information.

Description: This will have to be a task learners do after school. Encourage them to do the observation as soon as possible after the lesson – maybe the following weekend. Make sure they work in pairs or with a family member.

Learners will need to take the observation sheet and a pencil for writing and drawing. Suggest they take a clipboard as well. If they have a camera and/or binoculars they should take these as well.

Discuss in class where they can go and observe birds. Some learners may have a garden or access to someone's garden. Otherwise any local park or riverside or seaside place would be suitable.

Encourage learners to observe the birds on different visits and at different times. This will make them realise that the more observation they do the more data they will collect and therefore the more reliable their data will be. Refer to the New Science skills section at the end of the Learner's Book for an example of this. Tell the learners not to frighten the birds – they must be quiet and still so that the birds do not fly away.

They will also see that the same species of birds may eat different things at different times. In this way they will collect more reliable data from their observations.

Name of bird					
Circle the words which describe the habitat	Trees	Grass	Flowers	Water	Seawater
	Hot		Cold	Wet	Dry
Shape of beak (include a drawing)					
What is bird eating?					
Circle the type of bird you think it is	seed-eater fruit-eater		worm and insect eater water plant-eater		fish eater animal-eater

At least a week in advance, tell learners when they are to bring their completed observation sheets to class.

Try to have a bird reference book available for them to look up a bird they have seen.

Learners can present their results on a dot plot. A dot plot is an easy graph to draw and it gives a very clear picture of results or observations that are easy to interpret. At a glance you can see where there a many or few dots. Refer to the Skills Section at the end of the Learner's Book to show learners how to do this.

> **Digital Classroom:** If you have access to the Digital Classroom component, show the video 'Birds in different habitats' and ask the class these questions:

- What type of beak does this bird have?
- How does its beak help it to get food?
- What is the bird eating?
- What is the name of the bird?

> **Differentiation ideas:** This is an activity that learners can choose to do with a friend or a family member and they can get help with identifying the birds. So it should be possible for all levels.

> **Assessment ideas:** Let learners display their work and compare what they have discovered with other members of the class.

> **Reflection ideas:** Use the reflection questions in the Learner's Book. Tell learners to reflect on this activity and compare their feelings about how they could observe better next time and how they could use this skill in another situation, such as watching how animals behave either in real life or on a video.

3 Questions about plants surviving in places that are not their normal habitat (10 minutes)

Learning intention: Give examples of how plants can survive in a habitat that is not their natural one.

Resources: Learner's Book

Description: Show learners the photographs in the Learner's Book and discuss the answers in class.

4 Workbook 4.4: Focus, Practice and Challenge exercises (10 minutes each)

Learning intention: Identify features in the photographs and drawings and read information about how different animals are suited to their habitat, and answer questions.

Resources: Workbook 4.4

Description: Learners answer questions in the Workbook

> **Differentiation ideas:** The exercises become slightly more difficult as the learners work through the Workbook.

> **Assessment ideas:** You can set aside time to go through these exercises in class so that you can check that the learners have the correct answers.

5 Worksheet 4.4: Case study: Orangutans (15 minutes)

Learning intention: To find out the many ways that orangutans are suited to their habitat.

Resources: Worksheet 4.4 pack – there is a case study with a photograph, and three differentiated worksheets

Description: Learners read the case study material and answer the questions on the relevant worksheet.

> **Differentiation ideas:** Worksheet 4.4A provides help for learners with vocabulary and structured answers to questions, Worksheet 4.4B has general questions and more challenging questions are given in Worksheet 4.4C.

> **Assessment ideas:** Go through answers in class so that all learners can benefit

Plenary ideas

1 Activity 2: How are tigers suited to their habitat? (10 minutes)

Resources: Learner's Book

Description: Read the information about tigers to the learners. Explain any words they do not know, for example 'blend' (merge or match the surroundings) and 'striped' (bands of different colour, in this case yellow and dark brown). Learners can answer the questions in their notebooks.

2 Workbook 4.4: Focus exercise (10 minutes)

Resources: Workbook

Description: Show learners the photographs in the workbook and ask them to write their answers to the questions.

CROSS-CURRICULAR LINKS

Main teaching idea 4 and Worksheet 4.4 link to English – reading, writing and comprehension skills.

Homework ideas

Learners can do the exercises in the Workbook, or one of the Worksheets. For each, go through the answers at the beginning of your next lesson. You may like to give the learners the dot plot to draw for homework.

Check their dot plots by walking round the class and looking at each learner's dot plot at your next lesson.

Topic worksheets

Let all the learners read the case study text about the orangutan. Or you could read the text aloud in class.

Worksheet 4.4A

Give this to learners who have trouble with some of the vocabulary. It explains the key words and provides text for learners to fill in these words.

Worksheet 4.4B

Give this to learners who understand most of the text and appear more confident.

Worksheet 4.4C

Give this to confident learners who will have no problem with the text and can write their own sentences.

PROJECT: HOW PEOPLE USE VOLCANOES AND HOT SPRINGS

4SIC.04 Identify people who use science, including professionally, in their area and describe how they use science.

Discuss the topic for the project with the class. Discuss where there are volcanoes or hot springs in your area or in your country or a nearby country. Suggest how learners can find information – for example, a local tourist information office, farmers association or the internet.

Once learners have chosen their natural feature (volcano or hot spring) they must find information on how people use it (e.g. as a tourist destination, for farming, for a health spa). Then they can collect information and pictures and arrange these on an A4 sheet of paper.

Give learners a week or two before they have to hand in their poster. You can then display the posters in the classroom.

Project assessment

Learners can assess each other's work using questions such as these:

- How eye-catching is the poster?
- How interesting is the information?

- Does the poster link the natural feature to how it is used by people?
- Are the pictures relevant and interesting?

> 5 Light

Unit plan

Topic	Approximate number of learning hours	Outline of learning content	Resources
5.1 How we see things	1	• Investigate how we see a coin in a box and apply knowledge to other situations	**Learner's Book:** Think like a scientist: Investigate how we see an object Activity: How can the person see the car? **Workbook:** Topic 5.1 **Digital Classroom:** Song – Light fantastic!
5.2 Light travels in straight lines	1.5	• Prove that light travels in straight lines with a simple demonstration • Look at and practise drawing ray diagrams	**Learner's Book:** Think like a scientist: Prove that light travels in straight lines Activity: Practise drawing ray diagrams **Workbook:** Topic 5.2 ⬇ Worksheet 5.2
5.3 Light reflects off different surfaces	2.5	• Demonstrate how a mirror reflects light very well • Do a group Think like a scientist investigation to compare how well different surfaces reflect light, describe a pattern in results and make a conclusion	**Learner's Book:** Activity: Describe how people use mirrors to see things Think like a scientist: Investigate how well different surfaces reflect light **Workbook:** Topic 5.3 ⬇ Worksheets 5.3A, 5.3B and 5.3C
5.4 Light in the solar system	1	• Find out about what is in our solar system, answer questions and draw diagrams and do some research	**Learner's Book:** Activity: Planets in our solar system Think like a scientist: Find out what is in our solar **system** **Workbook:** Topic 5.4 ⬇ Worksheet 5.4A, 5.4B and 5.4C **Digital Classroom:** Video – Our solar system

Topic	Approximate number of learning hours	Outline of learning content	Resources
5.5 Day and night	1.5	• Use a globe as a model to demonstrate day and night, answer questions and complete a diagram	**Learner's Book:** Think like a scientist: Use a model to show day and night **Workbook:** Topic 5.5 **Digital Classroom:** Manipulative – Day and night
5.6 Investigating shadow lengths	2	• Carry out shadow stick investigation OR watch video of shadow stick experiment, draw results, describe a pattern in results and explain the apparent movement of the Sun throughout the day	**Learner's Book:** Think like a scientist: Investigate the changing length and position of a shadow **Workbook:** Topic 5.6 ⬇ Worksheet 5.6 **Digital Classroom:** Science Investigator video – How does the length and direction of a shadow change throughout the day?

Across unit resources

Learner's Book:

Project: Research the life and discoveries of an astronomer

Check your progress quiz

Teacher's Resource:

⬇ Language worksheets 1 & 2

⬇ End-of-unit test

⬇ Diagnostic check

⬇ Mid-point test

⬇ End-of-year **test**

Digital Classroom:

End-of-unit quiz

BACKGROUND KNOWLEDGE

Light

The main ideas for the first part of this unit are that light travels in straight lines from a source and we see objects because light reflects off objects into our eyes.

In Physics, light refers to electromagnetic radiation. The light we normally talk about in everyday life refers to the visible spectrum (the part of the electromagnetic spectrum that the human eye can see). Other animals can see different types of light. For example, dogs can see only shades of grey and some insects can see ultraviolet light.

Over the centuries, our ideas about light have changed dramatically. Pythagoras, best known for his theorem of the right-angled triangle, proposed that the way we see things resulted from light rays emerging from a person's eye and striking an object. We now know that this idea is incorrect.

Around 1000 C.E., an Arab mathematician and physicist called Alhazen demonstrated how the Sun is the source of light. Light from the Sun hits an object and then reflects from an object to the eyes of an observer. This is the correct explanation.

In this unit you will be discussing reflection. In reflection, a light ray strikes a smooth surface, such as a mirror, and bounces off. A reflected ray always comes off the surface of a smooth material at an angle equal to the angle at which the incoming ray hit the surface. In Physics, you'll hear this called the law of reflection. You've probably heard this law stated as 'the angle of incidence equals the angle of reflection'. Learners will only do this in Stage 7. In this stage they will draw ray diagrams showing the arriving ray and the reflected ray.

Solar system

In the second half of this unit you will be giving learners a 'taste' of astronomy when you discuss the solar system.

There are a lot of big concepts for learners to grasp. At this stage you do not teach learners about light years or gravity but you may find that some learners ask questions that will need this background information:

When any two objects are near to each other they produce a force that tries to pull them together. This force is called 'gravity' or 'gravitational force'. The bigger the object, the stronger the gravitational force it produces.

The force of gravity is what keeps objects in space moving in orbits around larger objects. If there was no gravity, objects would move in straight lines in space.

When any two objects are near to each other they produce a gravitational force that tries to pull them together. You will cover this in Stages 6 and 7.

Distances in space are very difficult to imagine. The Moon is about 500 times smaller than the Sun but the Moon and the Sun look about the same size to us. This is because the Sun is so much further away from us.

The distance between Earth and the Sun is about 150 million km. Astronomers call this distance an Astronomical Unit (AU) and it is used to express distances within the solar system.

A light year (ly) is the distance light travels in one year. Light travels at a speed of 3 000 000 km/sec, so a light year is about 9.5 trillion km. Astronomers measure distances in space in light years. When they see a star through a telescope they are seeing light that left that star several light years ago to reach Earth.

If you get into a discussion about light years with your learners, tell them that our nearest star, Alpha Centauri, is almost 4.4 ly away (about 40 trillion km).

TEACHING SKILLS FOCUS

Working in groups

In this unit there are several opportunities for groupwork.

Groupwork uses interactions between learners as part of the learning process. In this way learners are gaining important social skills as well as the science topic. Groupwork shares responsibility for learning among the learners. The learners may look to you as the teacher for help and information, but they can also seek help and information from each other.

One of the main advantages to groupwork is that it increases the opportunities for learner activities in big classes. Whether you have a large class or not, groupwork has many advantages:

- Interaction and working together – this provides an opportunity for learners to comment on each other's work, to criticise and provide each other with feedback.
- It helps improves their discussion and communication skills.
- Practice in their thinking and working scientifically skills.
- You can hold report back sessions.

Your role as the teacher

Before you begin the lesson it is very important to know how many groups you will have in your class so that you can have all the resources ready.

You could give each group a name. You could let learners choose their own group members or you could choose them yourself. If you keep the groups the same from one activity to the next it

has the advantage of learners getting to know how to work together. But if there are clashes it may be advisable to swap learners between groups.

Give groups a time limit so that they can plan accordingly.

It is important that you monitor group work while it is in progress. The challenge for you, as the teacher, is to be a good facilitator:

- Encourage equal participation from all group members.
- Make sure there is no abuse or ridicule within the group.
- Offer advice where necessary.
- Encourage the group when things are not going so well.
- Praise the group for the work they produce.

Assessing group work

Make sure that assessment covers not only results but the processes that led to the results, for example:

- how ideas are shared
- levels of participation
- strategies used for resolving conflict, helping each other, reaching agreement
- how influence is exerted
- what roles are adopted and how they help or hinder the group.

Try to put some of these ideas into practice during the course of this unit.

5.1 How we see things

LEARNING PLAN

Learning objectives	Learning intention	Success criteria
4Ps.03 Describe how objects which are not sources of light are seen.	• To investigate how we see things that are not sources of light.	• Learners can understand that they see an object because light reflects off the object into their eyes.

CONTINUED

Learning objectives	Learning intention	Success criteria
4TWSp.03 Make a prediction describing some possible outcomes of an enquiry.	• To be able to make predictions and see if results support our predictions.	• Learners can make a prediction and see if results support their predictions.
4TWSa.01 Identify if results support, or do not support, a prediction.	• To be able to make predictions and see if results support our predictions.	• Learners can make a prediction and see if results support their predictions.
4TWSa.03 Make a conclusion from results and relate it to the scientific question being investigated.	• To make a conclusion from our results.	• Learners can make a conclusion based on an investigation.

LANGUAGE SUPPORT

• **reflect** – the action of light bouncing off a surface

Get learners to use this word as often as possible as a verb, e.g. 'the light <u>reflects</u> off the object and into my eyes'. In English the word reflect can also mean 'to think deeply or to consider'. We use the noun 'reflection' in this book when we want learners to think and consider something they have done in the topic.

• **source** – where something comes from

In this context we are talking about sources of light such as the Sun or a lamp. Another example could be the source of water (a dam, a river, a reservoir, etc.).

Common misconceptions

Misconception	How to identify	How to overcome
Light travels out of our eyes to an object and this is how we see the object.	Ask learners to predict whether they will see the coin in the dark box in Think like a scientist: Investigate how we see an object. If they say yes they have the misconception.	Learners will only see the coin when the flashlight shines on it.

Starter ideas

1 Getting started (5–10 minutes)

Resources: Learner's Book; Digital Classroom song: Light fantastic (optional; you can play the whole song since it will revise what they already know about light, light sources, opaque and translucent and transparent objects and shadows)

Description: Ask learners the question in the Learner's Book. Discuss their answers in class.

> **Digital Classroom:** If you have access to the Digital Classroom component, use the song 'Light fantastic' to refresh learner's knowledge on light. The i button will explain how to use the song animation.

If learners answer question 3 as light travels from their eyes to the teacher, they do have the misconception. Tell them they are going to see that is not what happens in the activity that you are going to do.

2 What is outside? (5 minutes)

Resources: A view outside a window

Description: Ask learners to look out of the window. Ask these questions:

- What is the light source outside?
- What can you see?
- How can you see these things?

If learners answer that light travels from their eyes to the things outside, they do have the misconception outlined above. Tell them they are going to see that is not what happens in the activity that you are going to do.

Main teaching ideas

1 Think like a scientist: Investigate how we see an object (30 minutes)

Learning intentions: To investigate how we see things that are not sources of light; to make predictions and see if results support our predictions; to make a conclusion from our results.

Resources: Learner's Book; a cardboard box about 50 × 50 cm, a flashlight with batteries, a craft knife and a coin. If learners are cutting the holes, warn them to be careful when using the knife.

Description: Before you begin, ask learners what we mean when we predict something (say what you think is going to happen).

Demonstrate with one learner doing the instructions in the Learner's Book and the whole class answering the questions.

If possible, make three or four boxes with holes. Then each learner can take it in turns to carry out the steps.

Then learners answer questions 1–3 in the Learner's Book.

> **Practical guidance:** If you decide to do this activity as a demonstration you can cut the holes in the box lid before the lesson. Demonstrate with one learner doing the steps and the whole class answering the questions.

Safety warning: be careful when using the craft knife.

> **Differentiation ideas:** Ask learners to do the self-assessment in the Learner's Book to test their prediction skills.

2 Activity: How can the person see the car? (10 minutes)

Learning intention: Investigate how we see things that are not sources of light.

Success criteria: understand that I see an object because light reflects off the object into my eyes.

Resources: Learner's Book

Description: You could do this at the end of the lesson to consolidate what learners have learnt. Ask learners to write the answers to the first three questions in their notebooks.

Get learners to tell you their answers and then discuss question 4 in class.

> **Differentiation ideas:** All learners should be able to answer the questions. Those who find it difficult to write sentences can use the sentence in question 3 of the previous questions as a guide.

> **Assessment ideas:** Assess by discussing answers to the questions after this in a class discussion. You can also use the self-assessment questions in the Learner's Book.

3 Workbook 5.1: Focus, Practice and Challenge exercises (10–15 minutes)

Learning intention: Investigate how we see things that are not sources of light

Resources: Workbook 5.1

Description: Learners should answer the questions to the relevant exercise in the Workbook.

> **Differentiation ideas:** The Focus exercise is suitable for learners who need help with writing sentences.

The Practice exercise is suitable for learners who have understood the lesson well and can write their own sentences.

The Challenge exercise is good for learners who need a little more of a challenge.

> **Assessment ideas:** Assess by discussing answers in class.

Plenary ideas

1 Activity: How can the person see the car? (10 minutes)

Resources: Learner's Book

Description: See main teaching idea 2 for details.

> **Assessment ideas:** Learners could assess each other's answers for questions 1–3. Answer question 4 in class.

> **Reflection ideas:** Can I now answer the question 'How can I see my teacher?' correctly?

2 How can I see my partner? (5 minutes)

Resources: Pairs of learners

Description: Ask learners to get into pairs and look at each other.

Tell each learner to say 'I can see my partner because light…' (learner completes sentence).

The complete sentence should be similar to: 'I can see my partner because light from the lamp (or Sun) shines on my partner and reflects off my partner into my eyes.'

Homework ideas

1 Workbook 5.1 Focus exercise – an easy consolidation exercise.

2 Workbook 5.1 Practice or Challenge exercises – more difficult consolidation exercises.

Go through the answers in class at the start of your next lesson.

5.2 Light travels in straight lines

LEARNING PLAN

Learning objectives	Learning intention	Success criteria
4Ps.01 Know that light travels in straight lines and this can be represented with ray diagrams.	• To investigate how light travels.	• Learners can understand that light travels from a source in straight lines called rays.
4TWSp.03 Make a prediction describing some possible outcomes of an enquiry.	• To able to make a prediction about what will happen in an investigation.	• Learners can predict what will happen before we start an investigation.
4TWSa.01 Identify whether results support, or do not support, a prediction.	• To see if results support predictions.	• Learners can compare results with their predictions.
4TWSa.03 Make a conclusion from results and relate it to the scientific question being investigated.	• To be able to make a conclusion from our results.	• Learners can make a conclusion about how light travels.
4TWSm.03 Draw a diagram to represent a real-world situation and/or scientific idea.	• To be able to draw a ray diagram.	• Learners can label rays on a ray diagram and draw their own ray diagram to show how light travels.

LANGUAGE SUPPORT

- **proof** – scientific evidence that something is true (this is the noun)

- **prove** – to find proof that something is true when doing a scientific investigation (this is the verb)

- **ray** – a line that light travels in. We often talk about the Sun's rays

- **ray diagram** – a diagram to show how light travels. Learners will get plenty of practice drawing these in this Unit.

Common misconceptions

Misconception	How to identify	How to overcome
Light is everywhere so light can turn corners.	Learners' answers to question 3 of 'Getting started': Can light travel round corners?	Look at photographs of light rays in the Learner's Book and in the Think like a scientist investigation to show that light travels in straight lines.

Starter ideas

1 Getting started (5 minutes)

Resources: Learner's Book

Description: Look at the photographs in the Learner's Book and ask learners questions 1 and 2.

An incorrect answer to question 2 will identify if learners have the misconception that light can turn corners (correct answer: in a straight line).

2 Can we see around corners? (5 minutes)

Resources: Classroom and corridor

Description: Ask learners how we see another person (light travels to the person, light reflects off the person and into our eyes).

Now get one learner to stand by the door to the classroom. Ask:

Can we all see the learner? (Yes)

Will we see the learner if we open the classroom door and he walks down the corridor? (Yes/No)

Now open the door and tell the learner to walk a little way down the corridor. Ask: Can we see the learner now? (No)

An incorrect answer to question 2 will identify if learners have the misconception that light can turn corners.

Main teaching ideas

1 Think like a scientist: Prove that light travels in straight lines (30 minutes)

Learning intentions: Investigate how light travels; make predictions and see if results support predictions; make a conclusion from results.

Resources: Learner's Book; a cardboard or flexible plastic tube (it needs to bend without the tube closing) and a flashlight (with batteries) that fits over the hole in the tube.

If possible let learners try this for themselves in pairs – you will need several plastic tubes and flashlights. You could ask learners to bring these to school.

Description: Organise learners into pairs. Each pair has a plastic tube and a flashlight. Or learners can get into groups and take it in turns to use the plastic tube and flashlight.

Tell learners do follow the instructions in the Learner's Book and answer the questions as they go along.

> **Differentiation ideas:** Suitable for all learners.

2 Activity: Practise drawing ray diagrams (20 minutes)

Learning intention: Draw a ray diagram

Success criteria: label rays on a ray diagram and draw own ray diagram to show how light travels.

Resources: Learner's Book; a projector (optional)

Description: Project the drawings in the Learner's Book onto a screen or draw them on the white board.

Ask learners to answer all three questions in their notebooks. Then go through answers in class.

> **Differentiation ideas:** This will become evident when learners do the self-assessment. It will help you to decide which of the differentiated exercises in the Workbook and Worksheets are appropriate for each learner.

> **Assessment ideas:** Get learners to assess their progress in drawing ray diagrams in the self-assessment in the Learner's Book.

3   Workbook 5.2: Focus, Practice and Challenge exercises (10 minutes each)

Learning intention: Understand that light travels from a source in straight lines called rays.

Label rays on a ray diagram.

Resources: Workbook 5.2

Description: In the Focus exercise learners complete sentences by filling in missing words and draw rays on a diagram.

In the Practice exercise learners read a short story about Rabah and Khalid and then answer questions by completing a sentence and writing their own sentence. They then draw and label rays on a picture.

In the Challenge exercise learners read a short story about Marcus and Zara and then answer questions by drawing rays on a diagram.

> **Differentiation ideas:** The Focus exercise is suitable for learners still building confidence in this section or those who are not yet able to write in full sentences in English.

The Practice exercise is suitable for more confident learners since they have to apply knowledge to a new situation.

The Challenge exercise is for learners who need a more challenging activity.

Plenary ideas

1   Workbook 5.2: Focus, Practice and Challenge exercises (10 minutes each)

Resources: Workbook 5.2

Description: See main teaching idea 3 above

> **Assessment ideas:** You can set aside time at the beginning of the next lesson to assess their work.

Learners could mark each other's work while you walk around the class to sort out any problems. Or you can ask learners in turn to give you answers.

> **Reflection ideas:** It would be a good idea if learners answered the self-assessment questions in the Learner's Book when you finished the lesson and AGAIN after doing the Workbook exercises to see if they are more confident with more practice.

2   Worksheet 5.2 (10 minutes)

Resources: Worksheet 5.2

Description: Learners write and draw answers on the Worksheet using the Help or Stretch sheet as appropriate.

> **Assessment ideas:** Learners can assess their progress using the self-assessment questions in the Learner's Book.

Homework ideas

1   Learners can complete the Focus, Practice and Challenge exercises in the Workbook. You can set aside time at the beginning of the next lesson to assess homework. Learners could mark each other's work while you walk around the class to sort out any problems. Or you can ask learners in turn to give you answers.

2   Learners work through Worksheet 5.2. Learners can assess their progress using the self-assessment questions in the Learner's Book.

Topic worksheets

Worksheet 5.2: Light travels in straight lines

Learners study the images and draw and label rays on them.

All learners should be able to do the worksheet. Any learners that need help can use the Help sheet to answer worksheet questions 1–4. More confident learners can do Stretch questions 5 and 6 as well as worksheet questions 1–4.

Learners only need to do ONE option (i.e. with the Help sheet or with the Stretch questions), so they can choose which one to try.

5.3 Light reflects off different surfaces

LEARNING PLAN

Learning objectives	Learning intention	Success criteria
4Ps.02 Know that light can reflect off surfaces.	• To look at examples of how well a mirror reflects light.	• Learners can see a mirror reflects light very well.
4TWSp.02 Know there are five main types of scientific enquiry (research, **fair testing**, observing over time, identifying and classifying, and pattern seeking).	• To investigate how well light reflects off different surfaces and identify a pattern in results.	• Learners see how well light reflects off different surfaces and identify a pattern in results.
4TWSp.03 Make a prediction describing some possible outcomes of an enquiry.	• To be able to make predictions and see if results support the predictions.	• Learners can make predictions and see if results support their predictions.
4TWSa.01 Identify whether results support, or do not support, a prediction.	• To be able to make predictions and see if results support the predictions.	• Learners can make predictions and see if results support their predictions.
4TWSa.02 Describe simple patterns in results.	• To describe simple patterns in results.	• Learners can describe a pattern in results.
4TWSa.03 Make a conclusion from results and relate it to the scientific question being investigated.	• To make a conclusion related to how well different surfaces reflect light.	• Learners can make a conclusion about how well different surfaces reflect light.

LANGUAGE SUPPORT

- **absorb** – to take in a substance. For example, if you spill a liquid you can pat it with a paper towel. The paper towel absorbs the liquid

- **image** – a picture of the object that you see on a screen or in a mirror (learners will be familiar with looking at their image in a mirror)

- **mirror** – a very smooth, shiny surface that reflects light well

- **reflection** – when light bounces off a surface

- **surface** – the top layer that is next to the air (get learners to point to the surface of their desk or table)

Common misconceptions

Misconception	How to identify	How to overcome
Light ONLY reflects off mirrors.	Ask learners if they will be able to see their image in clear water. If they say no they have the misconception.	Use either of the Starter ideas or Think like a scientist investigation to show how well different surfaces reflect light.

Starter ideas

1 What can you see in the mirror and the aluminium foil? (5 minutes)

Resources: Small mirrors and aluminium foil

Description: Ask learners if they think they will see their reflection in the mirror and in the aluminium foil. If they say they will only see their reflection in the mirror they have the misconception above.

Tell learners to look in a mirror and a piece of aluminium foil and ask them if they can see their image in both surfaces. They will see their reflection in the aluminium foil but not as well as in the mirror.

2 Does light reflect off water? (5 minutes)

Resources: Large basin of clear water.

Description: Ask learners to look into the water – they should be able to see their reflection faintly in the water but not as well as in a mirror.

Main teaching ideas

1 Activity: Describe how people use mirrors to see things (10 minutes)

Learning intention: Know that light can reflect off surfaces.

Resources: Photographs in the Learner's Book.

Description: Discuss the photographs in class. Ask learners to tell you the answers to the questions. Help them where necessary. Encourage use of the words 'reflect', 'shiny', 'light' and 'source' in their answers.

> **Differentiation ideas:** The questions become more complex from 1 to 3.

2 Think like a scientist: Investigate how well different surfaces reflect light (30–40 minutes)

Learning intention: This addresses all the learning intentions listed in the table at the start of the topic.

Resources: Learner's Book; a selection of these materials: a mirror, a sheet of white paper, a ceramic tile, a cork tile, a sheet of aluminium foil, a metal saucepan lid, a sheet of clear plastic; a wooden chopping board, a white plastic chopping board.

Description:

Material	Reflection rating – prediction	Reflection rating – actual

First hold up each surface in turn and ask learners to predict how well they think the surface will reflect light. Learners record their predictions by filling in the middle column of their table and rating materials using the scale in their Learner's Book: 3: Perfect reflection 2: Fairly good reflection 1: Poor reflection 0: No reflection

Now set up the materials at eye height about a metre apart in a line so the learners can file past and look at each surface in turn.

Learners then complete the third column in their table.

To end the investigation learners answer the questions in the Learner's Book.

> **Practical guidance:** If you need extra materials, ask learners to bring some of the things to class in advance of the lesson.

> **Differentiation ideas:** This investigation is suitable for all learners.

> **Assessment ideas:** Use the self-assessment chart in the Learner's Book to allow learners to assess how well they can make predictions, test predictions and make a conclusion. They can reflect on whether they have improved since the last assessment. Make sure learners know that they have practised pattern seeking, which is one of the five types of scientific enquiry.

3 Workbook 5.3: Focus, Practice and Challenge exercises (10 minutes for each exercise)

Learning intention: In each exercise learners revise what they have learnt about light reflecting off surfaces.

In the Focus exercise the focus is on light reflecting off a mirror.

In the Practice exercise learners show that they can plan a fair test to investigate how well light reflects off different surfaces and describe simple patterns in results and make a conclusion.

In the Challenge exercise learners show that they understand how they can see something behind them using a mirror.

Resources: Workbook 5.3

Description: Give learners the exercises to do (see Differentiation ideas below for guidance). Learners answer the relevant questions in the Workbook.

> **Differentiation ideas:** Learners who have struggled with the concepts should start with the Focus exercise.

The Practice exercise is a good exercise for learners to revise what they know about fair testing. This would be a good exercise for all learners.

The Challenge exercise is a more challenging exercise for learners that need more stimulation.

> **Assessment ideas:** Assess the exercises at the beginning of the next lesson before you begin the new topic. Ask learners in turn to call out answers. If they have a wrong answer or an answer that could have alternatives ask learners for more suggestions. This method will give learners practice in assessing themselves.

Plenary ideas

1 Workbook 5.3: Focus exercise (10 minutes)

Resources: Workbook 5.3

Description: See main teaching idea 3

2 Self-assessment (5 minutes)

Resources: Self-assessment questions in the Learner's Book

Description: Learners can reflect on how well they can make and test a prediction and make a conclusion, and whether they feel they have improved and become more confident in these skills.

Homework ideas

1 Learners work through the Focus, Practice and Challenge exercises in the Workbook. Let learners choose which one they would like to start with. You can advise them if they are not sure. For example, if some learners have filled in the self-assessment answers and feel they are still not confident in the skills, advise them to do the Focus exercise.

Assess exercises at the beginning of the next lesson before you begin the new topic. Ask learners in turn to call out answers. If they have a wrong answer or an answer that could have alternatives, ask learners for more suggestions. This method will give learners practice in assessing themselves.

2 Learners can find materials at home, such as chopping boards, mirrors, and so on, and rate how well the materials reflect light. They can describe the pattern they observe.

5.4 Light in the solar system

LEARNING PLAN

Learning objectives	Learning intention	Success criteria
4ESs.03 Know that the Sun is the centre of our solar system.	• To discover that solar systems can contain stars, planets, asteroids and comets.	• Learners can show that the Sun is the centre of our solar system.
4ESs.02 Name the planets in our solar system.	• To name the planets in our solar system.	• Learners can name the planets in our solar system.
4ESs.04 Know solar systems can contain stars, planets, asteroids and comets.	• To discover that solar systems can contain stars, planets, asteroids and comets.	• Learners can describe the contents of solar systems as stars, planets, asteroids and comets.
4TWSm.02 Use models to show relationships, quantities, or scale.	• To use a model to show the relationship between bodies in the solar system.	• Learners can use a model to show relationships between bodies in the solar system.
4TWSm.03 Draw a diagram to represent a real-world situation and/or scientific idea.	• To draw a diagram of a moon orbiting a planet.	• Learners can draw a diagram of a moon orbiting a planet.
4TWSc.07 Use secondary information sources to research an answer to a question.	• To use reference material and the internet to find more information about the solar system.	• Learners can use reference books and the internet to find out more about the solar system.

LANGUAGE SUPPORT

- **asteroid** – a rocky mass that orbits the Sun. These are similar to planets but much smaller
- **closest** – the one that is nearest. For example, the closest shop from my home is just down our road
- **comet** – a lump of ice and dirt which moves in a large orbit around the Sun. Halley's comet (named after the astronomer Halley) takes 76 years to make one orbit around the Sun
- **furthest** – the one that is the most far away

- **orbit** – the movement of a body in space around a larger body in space. For example, the Earth moves around the Sun in an orbit. The Moon moves around the Earth in an orbit
- **solar system** – the Sun and the planets, moons, comets and asteroids which move around it. 'Solar' means Sun
- **spacecraft** – a vehicle for travelling in space. For example, a space shuttle is a spacecraft which takes scientists to and from the space centre

Common misconceptions

Misconception	How to identify	How to overcome
Earth has its own light	Third question in Getting started: What is the difference between a star and a planet? The correct answer is a star emits its own light and a planet reflects the star's light. Earth is a planet and the Sun is a star.	Photograph taken from space of the Earth and Moon lit by the Sun. The photograph shows half of the Earth lit up and half of the Moon lit up, each by another body – the Sun. The Earth would be totally lit up if it had its own source of light.

Starter ideas

1 Getting started (5 minutes)

Resources: Learner's Book

Description: Ask learners whether they can name the three ball-shaped objects in the photograph. Once these have been identified, ask learners to think about the relative sizes of these and what 'type' of object each of them is (a star, a planet or a moon). They can then give their answers to the three questions.

2 The Sun is our source of light (10 minutes)

Resources: Learner's Book

Description: Read the paragraph below the heading 'The Sun is our source of light' in the Learner's Book and discuss the photograph in class. Ask:

What colour is space? (Black)

Point to the space on the photograph. Ask: Where is Earth on the photograph? (Learners point to Earth)

Why is Earth only half lit up? (The half facing the Sun is lit up)

If Earth had its own light how much would be lit up? (The whole of Earth)

Point to the Moon. Ask: Why is only half of the Moon lit up? (The half facing the Sun is lit up)

To identify the misconception that Earth has its own light, show that space is black and that only half of the Earth and Moon are lit up by the Sun. If Earth had its own light (like the Sun) it would be totally lit up.

3 Starry night (5 minutes)

Resources: Tell learners to look at the night sky – best if far from city lights. In class you can show them a photograph of stars. You can source this on the internet or in a reference book.

Description: Ask questions: What colour is the sky? (Black)

What can you see? (Stars, Moon)

Why are the stars twinkling? (Stars all give out or emit light. The Sun is our star.)

Why is the Moon lit up? (It is lit up by the Sun.)

Only stars can give out light. The Sun is our star so it is our source of light. The Earth and the Moon reflect the Sun's light.

Main teaching ideas

1 Activity: Planets in our solar system (10–15 minutes)

Learning intention: Find out what is in our solar system.

Use a model to show the relationship between bodies in the solar system.

Resources: Learner's Book; Digital Classroom video: Our solar system (optional)

Description: Spend some time before learners do the activity discussing the diagram of the solar system.

> **Digital Classroom:** If you have access to the Digital Classroom component, show the video 'Our solar system'. The i button will explain how to use the video.

Remind learners that the diagram in the Learner's Book is a model of the solar system.

Ask learners why the diagram <u>is</u> a good model. (The Sun is in the centre. The Sun is the biggest body. The planets are in the correct order in distance from the Sun. All the planets are orbiting the Sun.)

Ask learners how the diagram is <u>not</u> a good model. (It is much smaller than the real thing. The Sun and planets are not drawn to scale. The distances are not drawn to scale.)

For consolidation tell learners to answer the questions in the Learner's Book.

> **Differentiation ideas:** All learners should be able to answer questions 1 and 2. Question 3 demands more understanding of the concepts.

> **Assessment ideas:** You can go through the answers when they have finished.

2 Questions on asteroids and moons (10 minutes)

Learning intention: Draw a diagram of a moon orbiting a planet.

Use reference material and the internet to find more information about the solar system.

Resources: Learner's Book; children's reference books on the solar system

Description: Read aloud the information in the Learner's Book about asteroids. Look at the photograph of an asteroid.

Ask learners: What shape is the asteroid? Is it round like a planet? (No)

Why is only half of the asteroid lit up? (Only the half facing the Sun is lit up.)

What is the black around the asteroid? (Empty space)

Look back to the diagram of the solar system in the Learner's Book and get learners to trace their finger round the Asteroid Belt and tell you where the planets Mars and Jupiter are.

Read aloud the information in the Learner's Book about moons. Look at our Moon on the satellite photograph at the beginning of the topic. Look at Titania in the photograph in the Learner's Book. Ask the class questions:

Why is only half of the Moon lit up? (Only the half facing the Sun is lit up.)

What is the black around the Moon? (Empty space)

Find planet Uranus on the diagram of the solar system.

If you have any children's reference books on the solar system you can show learners pictures of other asteroids and moons.

Then tell learners to answer questions 1–4. They can write their answers in their notebooks. You may want learners to finish questions 5 and 6 for homework since they need access to the internet or a reference book for question 6.

> **Practical guidance:** Give learners time to do this activity in class. Walk around and help learners if they need it. Go through answers in class before you carry on with the lesson.

> **Differentiation ideas:** All learners should be able to answer questions 1–3 because the answers are in the text. Question 4 will show you if there are any learners who have still not overcome the misconception.

Question 5 is good practice for showing an answer in a drawing.

To answer question 6, learners need to look on the internet (search for the question 'How many moons does Jupiter have?') or use a reference book.

3 Think like a scientist: Find out what is in our solar system (10–15 minutes)

Learning intention: Know that solar systems can contain stars, planets, asteroids and comets.

Use a model to show the relationship between bodies in the solar system.

Draw a ray diagram.

Use reference material and the internet to find more information about the solar system.

Resources: Learner's Book

Description: Read aloud the text on comets. Tell learners that comets move in orbits around the Sun but their orbits are not the same as the planet's orbits. Comets' orbits are huge so we rarely see one. For example, Halley's comet only comes past Earth once every 76 years.

To end the lesson learners can answer the questions. They will need the internet or reference books to answer questions 4 and 5 so they may need to do these questions at home.

> **Differentiation ideas:** All learners should be able to answer questions 1–2 because the answers are in the text. Question 3 is good practice drawing a ray diagram in a different context to the ray diagrams they drew before. Some learners may need help with this.

To answer questions 4 and 5 learners need to look on the internet (search for the question) or use a reference book.

4 Workbook 5.4: Focus, Practice and Challenge exercises (10–12 minutes each)

Learning intention: Know that the Sun is the centre of our solar system.

Name the planets in our solar system.

Know solar systems can contain stars, planets, asteroids and comets.

Use models to show relationships, quantities, or scale.

Describe how scientific knowledge and understanding changes over time through the use of evidence gained by enquiry (Challenge exercise).

Resources: Workbook 5.4

Description: Give learners the exercises to do (see 'Differentiation ideas' below for guidance). Learners answer the relevant questions in the Workbook.

> Differentiation ideas: Focus exercise: suitable for learners who have struggled to concept of orbits and what body moves around which other body.

Practice exercise: suitable for all learners.

Challenge exercise: mainly for learners who have grasped everything in the topic and need some new stimulus material to work with.

> Assessment ideas: Go through answers in class at the beginning of your next lesson. This will be good consolidation before going on to the next topic.

5 Worksheets 5.4A, 5.4B or 5.4C (20 minutes)

Learning intention: Know that the Sun is the centre of our solar system.

Name the planets in our solar system.

Know solar systems can contain stars, planets, moons.

Draw a diagram to represent a real-world situation and/or scientific idea (Worksheet 5.4B).

Resources: Worksheet pack

Description: Each worksheet has the same case study for learners to read. Learners then answer the questions on the worksheet they have been given (depending on their need – see 'Differentiation ideas' below.

> Differentiation ideas: Worksheet 5.4A has simple questions needing short answers.

Worksheet 5.4B develops skills and contains more difficult questions, and learners have to draw a diagram.

In Worksheet 5.4C, learners have to make a comparison of planets Earth and Jupiter and record their answers in a table.

Plenary ideas

1 Workbook 5.4: Focus exercise (10–15 minutes)

Resources: Workbook 5.4

Description: See main teaching idea 4.

> Assessment ideas: Go through answers in class at the beginning of your next lesson. This will be good consolidation before going on to the next topic.

2 Workbook 5.4: Challenge exercise (10 minutes)

Resources: Workbook 5.4

Description: This exercise is suitable for learners that have understood everything in the topic and need extra stimulus.

> Assessment ideas: Go through answers in class at the beginning of your next lesson.

CROSS-CURRICULAR LINKS

Main teaching idea 5 links with Maths – measurement of time.

Homework ideas

1 Learners can complete the Practice exercise in the Workbook.

2 Learners work through Worksheet 5.4A, 5.4B or 5.4C, according to learner's confidence level.

Topic worksheets

Worksheet 5.4A: Jupiter

Learners read a case study about Jupiter and answer simple questions needing short answers.

Worksheet 5.4B: Jupiter

Learners read a case study about Jupiter and answer more difficult questions and draw a diagram.

Worksheet 5.4C: Jupiter

Learners read a case study about Jupiter and to make a comparison of planets Earth and Jupiter and record their answers in a table.

5.5 Day and night

Learning objectives	Learning intention	Success criteria
4ESs.01 Explain why the spinning of the Earth on its axis leads to the apparent movement of the Sun, night and day (and changes in shadows).	• To explain what causes night and day.	• Learners can understand that the Earth's spinning on its axis causes night and day.
4TWSm.02 Use models to show relationships, quantities, or scale.	• To be able to use a globe as a model to show night and day.	• Learners can use a globe as a model to show night and day.
4TWSm.03 Draw a diagram to represent a real-world situation and/or scientific idea.	• To draw a diagram to represent day and night.	• Learners can complete and label a diagram to show day and night.

LANGUAGE SUPPORT

- **anticlockwise** – the opposite of clockwise which is the direction the hands of the clock move

- **axis** – anything that spins or rotates has to turn around a central line. This line is the axis. However, in this topic we use the Earth's axis often in diagrams. This can be confusing for learners because, although we have said it is an imaginary line, they may think the axis really does stick out of the Earth at both ends!

- **globe** – we use this word in this topic to describe the model of the Earth. However, in everyday life you often hear people talking about the globe meaning the whole world. The adjective 'global' is also widely used, for example global warming, global wars

- **spin** – a verb that means to turn very fast. The best example of this is a spinning top

- **tilted** – at an angle, not vertical

Common misconceptions

Misconception	How to identify	How to overcome
The Sun moves across the sky every day and this is what causes day and night.	Both starter ideas have questions which will show you which learners have this misconception.	Go through starter idea 2 and main teaching idea 1.

Starter ideas

1 Getting started (5–10 minutes)

Resources: Learner's Book

Description: Ask learners questions in the Learner's Book.

When you ask learners where the Sun rises in the morning get them to try to relate this to where they are at school – e.g. which side of the school does the Sun rise? Do the same for the sunset. Then ask what does the Sun do between sunrise and sunset? Some learners will say it moves across the sky – this shows they have the misconception. Others will remember that it appears to move across the sky.

Then ask them: What does move? Some may say the Earth. In this lesson you will show this to be true.

2 A model to show the Sun does not move (10 minutes)

Resources: A table lamp and 6 learners

Description: Place the lamp on a table and turn it on. This represents the Sun shining. Get the learners to stand in a circle with everyone facing outwards. The circle of learners represents the Earth. Move slowly round so that each person faces the Sun in turn. Keep moving until you reach the spot where you started. Collect evidence to support the idea that the Earth moves throughout the day and not the Sun.

Observe when you are facing the Sun, when the Sun is on your left side, on your right side and when you can't see the Sun at all.

Before you start, ask learners whether they think the Sun moves across the sky during the day. Even if some learners say it doesn't or it appears to move but it doesn't really, they may not be convinced. This short demonstration should help to convince them that the Sun does not move but the Earth does.

Main teaching ideas

1 Think like a scientist: Use a model to show day and night (10 minutes)

Learning intentions: To explain what causes night and day; to use a globe as a model to show night and day; to draw a diagram to represent day and night.

Resources: Learner's Book; a globe, a piece of sticky tape and a flashlight.

Description: Before you do this activity introduce the learners to the globe as a model of the Earth. Use the text in the Learner's Book to point out the axis. Explain that the axis is an imaginary 'stick' passing through the Earth from the North Pole to the South Pole and that it is tilted. The tilt of the axis will become very important next year when you move on to explain how we have seasons, so it is good to introduce it now. Then demonstrate on the globe that it is around this axis that the Earth spins.

You should also explain the term anticlockwise because this is the direction in which the Earth spins. This is important because it affects time differences between one part of the world and another.

Learners will be amazed at how fast the Earth spins.

Then stick the piece of sticky tape on your country on the globe. Follow the instructions in the Learner's Book. Get one learner to hold the globe and another to hold the flashlight (the Sun). Spin the globe and shout 'Day!' when your country is having day and 'Night!' when it is having night.

When you are sure learners have got the idea of the Earth spinning causes day and night, tell them to answer the questions. They can work in pairs but write down their answers. In question 1 they must complete a sentence. In question 2 they complete a diagram. Questions 3 and 4 are more difficult – see below in Differentiation ideas.

> **Differentiation ideas:** All learners should be able to answer question 1 correctly.

With question 2 make sure the learners have shaded in the Earth correctly. Some may have shaded up to the axis.

Questions 3 and 4 are more challenging. Question 3 will test that learners know which direction the Earth is spinning AND that they know where Malaysia and Spain are!

Question 4 shows how life could be very different if the Earth took a much shorter time to spin.

> **Assessment ideas:** Use learners' answers to questions to assess their understanding:

Can learners:

* show by shading in a diagram correctly that Earth spinning on its axis causes day and night?

* understand that Earth spins anticlockwise and this causes places in the east to be ahead of places in the west in time?

* understand that the length of time a planet takes to make one complete turn tells us how long the day and night is?

2 Workbook 5.5: Focus, Practice and Challenge exercises (10 minutes each)

Learning intentions: To explain what causes night and day; to use a diagram as a model to show night and day; to compare Earth's night and day with other planets.

Resources: Workbook 5.5

Description: Give learners appropriate exercises to do (see 'Differentiation ideas' below for guidance). Learners answer the relevant questions in the Workbook.

> **Differentiation ideas:** The Focus exercise is suitable for all learners.

The Practice exercise requires that learners write sentences for some of the answers. This exercise also uses different planets to demonstrate day and night so learners have to apply their knowledge to a different situation.

The Challenge exercise is more difficult. Information is given as data in a table about spin times on different planets. Learners must apply their knowledge to different planets and also get information from a table to answer the questions.

Plenary ideas

1 Who is having day and who is having night? (5 minutes)

Resources: Globe, stickers

Description: Get learners into groups of four. Learner 1 is the Sun. Learner 2 holds the globe. Learner 3 puts different coloured stickers on two different countries on different sides of the globe. Learner 4 says which country is having day (the country facing the 'Sun') and which country is having 'night' (the country facing away from the 'Sun'). Then Learner 2 spins the globe a little. Now which country is having

day and which is having night? Then they can change roles and put stickers on different countries.

2 Digital Classroom manipulative: Day and night (5–10 minutes)

Resources: Digital classroom manipulative: Day and night

Description: If you have access to the Digital Classroom component, use the manipulative 'Day and night' to consolidate learners' understanding. The i button will explain how to use the manipulable. Learners should answer the questions as they come up on the screen.

CROSS-CURRICULAR LINKS

Main teaching idea 1 links to Geography or Social Studies.

Main teaching idea 2 links to Geography or Social Studies, Maths – fractions and time measurement.

Homework ideas

1 Explain what causes day and night to a person at home.

Timing: 15 minutes

Resources: Learners must choose what to use for their model. They can use a globe or a ball of wool or soft ball that is able to turn and a flashlight.

Description: Assemble the 'Earth ' and its axis. Make sure it can turn on its axis. Get the person to whom you are explaining the concept to hold the 'Sun'.

> **Assessment ideas:** learners copy and complete this self-assessment grid:

Can I explain to somebody else:	Very well	Quite well	I need more practice
which parts of my model represent the Earth and the Sun?			
how the Earth spins on my model?			
what causes day and night?			

2 Learners complete the Focus, Practice and Challenge exercises in the Workbook.

5.6 Investigating shadow lengths

Learning objectives	Learning intention	Success criteria
4ESs.01 Explain why the spinning of the Earth on its axis leads to the apparent movement of the Sun, night and day, and change in shadows.	• To be able to explain changes in shadows in terms of Earth spinning on its axis.	• Learners can explain, in terms of the apparent movement of the Sun, changes in shadows in the shadow stick investigation.
4TWSp.03 Make a prediction describing some possible outcomes of an enquiry.	• To be able to make predictions and identify if results support predictions.	• Learners can make predictions before carrying out an investigation and see whether their predictions are correct or not.
4TWSa.01 Identify whether results support, or do not support, a prediction.	• To be able to make predictions and identify if results support predictions.	• Learners can make predictions before carrying out an investigation and see whether their predictions are correct or not.
4TWSp.02 Know there are five main types of scientific enquiry (research, fair testing, observing over time, identifying and classifying, and **pattern seeking**).	• To be able to measure the lengths of shadows and describe simple patterns in results.	• Learners can describe patterns in results.
4TWSa.03 Make a conclusion from results and relate it to the scientific question being investigated.	• To be able to make a conclusion from results.	• Learners can make a conclusion about how shadows change throughout the day from results.
4TWSc.08 Collect and record observations and/or measurements, in tables and diagrams.	• To be able to measure the lengths of shadows, record in a table.	• Learners can measure and record lengths of shadows throughout the day.
4TSWa.04 Present and interpret results using tables, bar charts and dot plots.	• To be able to draw a dot plot.	• Learners can draw a dot plot of shadow lengths.

LANGUAGE SUPPORT

• **apparent movement** – this means that the movement does not really happen but it looks like it happens

We use the phrase 'apparent movement of the Sun' to describe how we see the Sun 'moving' from one side of the sky to the other, but with our science knowledge we know that the Sun does not really move, it is the Earth that moves.

Common misconceptions

Misconception	How to identify	How to overcome
The Sun moves across the sky.	Show photos of a golf flag at different times of day. Ask learners why they think the shadow changes at different times of the day. If they say it is because the Sun moves across the sky they have the misconception.	Explain these changes in shadows using what they learnt in the previous topic, that Earth spins on its axis once every 24 hours and <u>not</u> that the Sun moves across the sky.

Starter ideas

1 Getting started (5 minutes)

Resources: Learner's Book

Description: Learners look at the picture in the Learner's Book. Ask the three questions and get different learners to give you the answers.

To identify if learners hold the misconception that the Sun moves across the sky, ask a fourth question: Do you think these shadows will change during the day?

Learners may say yes. If so, then see if they can suggest if they get longer or shorter and if they change in direction.

Then ask: Why do you think the shadows change? The correct answer is that the Earth spins on its axis which causes the Sun to appear to be in different parts of the sky and this is why the shadows change. But you will find this out during the lesson. If learners say the Sun moves it means they still have the misconception. You must remind them that we proved this was not the case in the last topic.

2 Shadow lengths questions (5 minutes)

Resources: Learner's Book

Description: Look at the photographs of the shadows at midday and late afternoon. Ask the questions in the Learner's Book.

If they have the misconception that the Sun moves they will answer question 4 by saying the Sun moves across the sky during the day.

Main teaching ideas

1 Think like a scientist: Investigate the changing length and position of a shadow (40 minutes)

Some of the readings will have to be made at different times of day and not during your lesson. You will have to assign different learners to go and make these readings and then gather all the readings together the following day.

If you decide to use the Digital Classroom investigation video, it will take 10 minutes. This includes time taken for class to answer questions on the screen. We suggest you play it twice.

Learning intentions: To investigate how shadows change in length throughout the day; make predictions and identify if results support our predictions; measure the lengths of shadows, record in a table and describe simple patterns in results; make a conclusion from results.

Resources: Learner's Book; a sunny day, a stick about 20 cm high, a sheet of white paper, some modelling clay, four stones, a ruler, a marker pen; Digital Classroom Science Investigator video: How does the length and direction of a shadow change throughout the day? (optional)

Description: Early in the morning choose a place in full sunlight (where there are no shadows nearby) to set up your stick. Push the stick into the ground or stick it upright with modelling clay.

Show the learners how a shadow of the stick falls on the paper. Mark the end of the shadow on the paper with a marker pen and write the time. Observe where the Sun appears to be in the sky (tell learners not to look directly at the Sun as they will damage their eyes). Ask learners to predict how they think the shadow will change in direction and length throughout the day.

Get learners to volunteer to return to the shadow stick every hour until the end of school. Each time they mark the end of the shadow on the paper with a marker pen and write the time. Observe whether the Sun is higher or lower in the sky and whether it appears to have moved sideways. Decide whether the change was as they predicted or not.

Go to the shadow stick yourself to accompany learners when possible. You should go for the last recording of the day to collect the stick and the paper and bring it back to class.

At the beginning of the next lesson join the dots you made for the ends of the shadows to the hole where the stick was. These are your shadow lines. Measure the length of each shadow line with a ruler. Record the lengths of the shadows in a table alongside the times.

Encourage learners to repeat this investigation over several days using a different sheet of paper each day.

Some days will be cloudy and they will not get a complete set of observations of shadows. By doing the investigation several times they see that the more observations you do, the more reliable your data are.

In class discuss the answers to the questions in the Learner's Book. Learners do not need to write them down. They can practise written answers later in the exercises. Try to get different learners to answer each time.

> **Digital Classroom:** If you have access to the Digital Classroom component, show the Science Investigator video 'How does the length and direction of a shadow change throughout the day?' to the learners. The i button will explain how to use the video.

> **Practical guidance:** Make sure learners do not look straight at the Sun. This will damage their eyes.

> **Differentiation ideas:** The more you involve the learners in this activity, the more likely they are to understand the pattern of the shadows and the final explanation. They can assess their own progress with these skills using this grid:

How well can I:	Very well	Not very confident	I need more practice in this
Describe a pattern in results?			
Give a scientific explanation for a pattern in result?			

If you are using the video, play it twice so that more learners can have a chance to answer the on-screen questions.

2 Workbook 5.6: Focus, Practice and Challenge exercises (10 minutes each)

Learning intentions: To predict how shadows change; to describe simple patterns in results; to make a conclusion from results; to understand that shadows change in length and direction throughout the day because of the apparent movement of the Sun caused by Earth spinning on its axis.

Resources: Workbook 5.6

Description: Learners work through and answer the relevant questions in the Workbook.

> **Differentiation ideas:** All learners should be able to do the Focus exercise. Most learners will not find the Practice exercise too difficult.

In the Challenge exercise, learners must apply what they have found out in the shadow stick investigation to a new situation, so this exercise is more difficult.

3 Worksheet 5.6 (10 minutes)

Learning intentions: To identify a pattern in results; to draw a graph; to make predictions (Stretch sheet).

Resources: Worksheet 5.6.

Description: Learners answer questions and complete or draw a graph on the Worksheet

> **Differentiation ideas:** The Help sheet provides help to draw the line graph (axes and scales provided). In the Stretch sheet learners have extra questions to answer which demand more lateral thinking.

Plenary ideas

1 Digital Classroom Science Investigator video: How does the length and direction of a shadow change throughout the day? (if not shown earlier in lesson) (10 minutes)

Resources: Digital Classroom Science Investigator video: How does the length and direction of a shadow change throughout the day?

Description: Play the Digital Classroom Science Investigator video 'How does the length and direction of a shadow change throughout the day?' and get learners to answer the on-screen questions.

2 Worksheet 5.6 (10 minutes)

Resources: Worksheet 5.6

Description: This worksheet gives learners the opportunity to present data from a changing shadow length investigation in a line graph. There is a Help sheet for drawing the line graph (with axes and scales provided), and some Stretch questions where learners must predict further results. Distribute the Help sheet and Stretch questions according to learners' abilities.

> **Assessment ideas:** Learners can assess their graphs using the grid provided on the Worksheet.

> **Reflection ideas:** Am I sure that I understand that the Sun only appears to move across the sky?

The main objective of this topic is that learners really understand that the Earth spinning on its axis causes shadows to change in length and direction throughout the day. The apparent movement of the Sun does make this difficult for some learners, but it is important that you keep on referring back to the demonstrations in the previous topic.

CROSS-CURRICULAR LINKS

Main teaching idea 1 links to Maths: measuring time.

Main teaching idea 3 links to Maths: drawing dot plots.

Homework ideas

1 Learners work through the Focus, Practice and Challenge exercises in the Workbook. Learners should choose which exercise to start with according to their ability. (see notes in main teaching idea 3).

2 If learners have not done the Worksheet in class they should do this for homework. Go through answers in class at the beginning of your next lesson.

Topic worksheets

Worksheet 5.6: Investigating shadow lengths

All learners should be able to do the worksheet. Any learners that need help can use the Help sheet to answer worksheet question 1. More confident learners can do the Stretch questions.

PROJECT: RESEARCH THE LIFE AND DISCOVERIES OF AN ASTRONOMER

4SIC.01 Describe how scientific knowledge and understanding changes over time through the use of evidence gained by enquiry.

Read the text in the Learner's Book about how scientists discovered the solar system in the Learner's Book. Explain any words the learners do not understand.

Learners will discover that the earliest astronomers were from Africa and India. Many years ago scientists thought that the Earth was flat. And that the Earth remained still while the Sun and the planets moved around it. It was only when telescopes were invented that astronomers could actually see which bodies were moving.

Learners can work in pairs for this project. Their task is to choose one of the astronomers highlighted in the text and find more information on them. They can use children's reference books and/or the internet.

They should make a list of the headings in the Learner's Book and fill in information when they find it in their internet search or reference book.

If possible find some pictures of the person or a diagram of what they were suggesting.

Give learners at least a week to do their project. Then they can present their information in class using the notes they have made. Each presentation should not take longer than three minutes.

Assessment for presentation

You can assess learners using a grid like this:

Did learners:	Yes	Partly	No
speak clearly?			
work together?			
find interesting information?			
find interesting pictures?			
keep to 3 minutes?			

>6 Electricity

Unit plan

Topic	Approximate number of learning hours	Outline of learning content	Resources
6.1 Which materials conduct electricity?	2	• Review a simple circuit • Make a simple circuit and test a variety of materials to see if they conduct electricity	**Learner's Book:** Think like a scientist: Test which materials conduct electricity **Workbook:** Topic 6.1 ⬇ Worksheet 6.1 **Digital Classroom:** Song – You've got to have a circuit! Activity – Which materials conduct electricity?
6.2 Does water conduct electricity?	1	• Teacher demonstration to investigate whether water conducts electricity	**Learner's Book:** Think like a scientist: Investigate whether water conducts electricity **Workbook:** Topic 6.2 **Digital Classroom:** Science Investigators video – Does water conduct electricity?
6.3 Using conductors and insulators in electrical appliances	1	• Review previous work on electrical appliances and safety • Teacher to show plugs, electrical wiring and appliances such as an iron to show where electrical conductors and insulators are used	**Learner's Book:** Activity 1: Classify materials used in electrical appliances as electrical conductors or insulators Activity 2: Predict safe or unsafe use of appliances **Workbook:** Topic 6.3 ⬇ Worksheet 6.3A, 6.3B and 6.3C **Digital Classroom:** Song – There's electricity
6.4 Switches	1.5	• Make a switch from a wood block, metal paper clip and metal drawing pins. Show how it opens and closes a circuit	**Learner's Book:** Think like a scientist 1: Make a switch Think like a scientist 2: Make a circuit with a switch **Workbook:** Topic 6.4 ⬇ Worksheet 6.4A, 6.4B and 6.4C

Topic	Approximate number of learning hours	Outline of learning content	Resources
6.5 Changing the number of components in a circuit	2	• Investigate what happens when the number of components in a circuit is changed. Ideally this should be a group activity.	**Learner's Book:** Think like a scientist: What happens when we change the number of components in a circuit? **Workbook:** Topic 6.5 **Digital Classroom:** Science Investigator video – What happens when we change the number of components in a circuit?

Across unit resources

Learner's Book:

Project: Batteries

Check your progress quiz

Teacher's Resource:

⬇ Language worksheets 1 & 2

⬇ End-of-unit test

⬇ Diagnostic check

⬇ Mid-point test

⬇ End-of-year test

Digital Classroom: End-of-unit quiz

BACKGROUND KNOWLEDGE

To introduce this concept, you could refer back to the particle model (see in the Learner's Book). Remind learners that all matter is made up of particles. Each substance is made up of very small particles that we can't see, even under a microscope. These are atoms that they will learn about later in their education. Each atom is made up of even smaller particles. Some of these particles have a negative charge (electrons) and some have a positive charge (protons). Sometimes charged particles escape from their atoms.

Current can be thought of as the flow of particles around a circuit. For the purposes of understanding the science at this stage, current flows from the positive to the negative terminal of a cell. In reality, electrons are flowing in the opposite direction, but that is beyond what learners need to know at this stage.

Some types of atoms lose their electrons more easily than others, and these materials conduct electricity better than those whose electrons are not lost as easily. Copper is a well-known example of such a material. This is why we use copper wires to carry or conduct electricity in a circuit.

On the other hand, plastic, wood, paper and cork are formed of carbon. Carbon atoms have a very stable structure and do not lose electrons easily. This is why these materials are insulators of electricity.

CONTINUED

In Topic 6.2 learners discover that pure water does not conduct electricity, but water with salts dissolved in it does conduct electricity. The atoms of molecules in pure water have a stable structure so pure water does not conduct electricity. But as soon as you add salts to water it does conduct electricity because the atoms in molecules of salts are charged (they are called ions). They break away from each other when they dissolve in the water and they are freely moving charged particles.

Charged particles are inside the copper wires, but we need something to push these particles around the circuit. This is where the cell comes in. The cell contains chemicals which react with each other and give off chemical energy. This energy provides the 'push' to move the charged particles around the circuit. In Topic 6.3, you will introduce the idea of the strength of electricity or voltage. A cell has a certain voltage and, when it has used up all the chemicals (a 'flat' cell), it does not give out any more chemical energy and the electricity stops going around the circuit. You do not have to say any more about voltage at this stage, but it is worth mentioning, if only because learners need to know what the V stands for on batteries and appliances.

In Topic 6.3 you introduce mains electricity, which has a much stronger voltage. This needs big generators to push it around circuits. The generators are in power stations. Cables on pylons carry the electricity from the power stations to homes, factories and industries.

Learners may think that electricity is only something that we use in circuits. It is important that they know that electricity exists naturally everywhere. It exists throughout space because of the loose electrons in space. Lightning is one form of natural electricity that you can see. Inside our bodies, our thoughts are really little spurts of electricity that travel along our nerves and between cells in our brain. It is only in the last two hundred years that people have learned to use electricity for their own purposes, to run machines.

TEACHING SKILLS FOCUS

Skills for life: Safety in a Science classroom

The number one priority in any Science classroom is the safety of the learners. In your role as the teacher, it is up to you to ensure there is a safe environment in which your learners can investigate the Science topics they are learning about and gain practical Science skills.

You might like to set up some general safety rules for the class, such as tying long hair back or following instructions carefully. You could ask the learners for suggestions. And you can refer to the Science Skills section at the end of the Learner's Book. This not only encourages them to own the rules and therefore follow them when inside and outside the classroom, but also promotes taking ownership for their own learning regarding safety and keeping themselves and others around them safe. You should go over the safety rules regularly to ensure this becomes second nature to the students.

Before starting any of the practical activities given in the Learner's Book or Teacher's Resource, you should go through any specific safety risks for the activity with the learners. Ensure they understand what these are, when they might encounter them and what they should do if things go wrong.

In this unit your learners will be working with electricity. It is really important to make them aware of how to work with electricity safely.

They come across mains electricity for the first time in Topic 6.3 – 110V or 220V is a lot different to 1.5V or 3V, which you use in the classroom activities.

You should go through the following safety points when starting this unit. You could add them to your general list of safety points for the classroom:

- Never put fingers or other objects in a plug.

- Never use anything with a cord or plug around water.

- Never pull a plug out by its cord.

- Watch out for plastic insulation that's worn away and exposed bare wires in electric cords.

- Store bathroom and kitchen appliances like hair driers out of reach of small children who are curious and might try to play with them.

CONTINUED

The information about safety that you give to the students will be a life skill which they can take home and tell their family about. Maybe they have some unsafe wires or appliances at home that they can warn their parents about! They can teach younger siblings how to use appliances safely such as never handling live appliances with wet hands and always turning the switch off when they have finished using an appliance. They can look at home to check that there are no damaged electric cords which could lead to electric shocks or fires.

This life skill also extends beyond the classroom and home environments into the wider world. When learners are outside, walking to school perhaps, they will pass overhead power lines. These can be extremely dangerous because the voltage is very high (see Workbook 6.3). Warn them to stay away from broken and fallen power lines.

lines and don't fly kites close to power lines!

Get learners to talk about power lines they see and explain how important it is to keep well away from them.

In Topic 6.2 learners will find out that water (except pure water) is a conductor of electricity. This is why we can get electric shocks because our bodies contain a lot of water. This brings up further, wider safety issues such as not swimming when there is an electric storm. Workbook 6.2 has a good story about this issue.

Challenge yourself to make safety a regular part of your lessons, particularly during the set-up of any practical activities. Afterwards, ask yourself:

- What are your overall thoughts? Are they mainly positive or negative?
- What were the most interesting discoveries you made?
- What were the most challenging moments?

6.1 Which materials conduct electricity?

LEARNING PLAN

Learning objectives	Learning intention	Success criteria
4Pe.04 Know some materials are good electrical conductors, especially metals, and some are good electrical insulators.	• To be able to use a fair test to group objects into conductors and insulators of electricity.	• Learners can use a circuit to make a fair test to group materials into conductors and insulators of electricity and test their predictions.
4TWSp.02 Know that there are five main types of scientific enquiry (research, **fair testing**, observing over time, identifying and **classifying**, and **pattern seeking**).	• To be able to use a fair test to group objects into conductors and insulators of electricity.	• Learners can use a circuit to make a fair test to group materials into conductors and insulators of electricity and test their predictions.
4TWSp.03 Make a prediction describing some possible outcomes of an enquiry.	• To be able to make predictions and identify if results support predictions or do not support predictions.	• Learners can predict which materials will be conductors and insulators of electricity.
4TWSa.01 Identify whether results support, or do not support, a prediction.	• To be able to make predictions and identify if results support predictions or do not support predictions.	• Learners can identify if results support predictions or do not support predictions.

CONTINUED

Learning objectives	Learning intention	Success criteria
4TWSc.01 Use observations and tests to sort, group and classify objects.	• To be able to use a fair test to group objects into conductors and insulators of electricity.	• Learners can use a circuit to make a fair test to group materials into conductors and insulators of electricity and test their predictions.
4TWSa.02 Describe simple patterns in results.	• To be able to describe simple patterns in results and make a conclusion from results.	• Learners can identify a pattern in results.
4TWSa.03 Make a conclusion from results and relate it to the scientific question being investigated.	• To be able to describe simple patterns in results and make a conclusion from results.	• Learners can make a conclusion from results.
4TWSa.04 Present and interpret results using tables, bar charts and dot plots.	• To be able to draw a dot plot to present results.	• Learners can draw a dot plot to present their results.
4TWSa.05 Identify risks and explain how to stay safe during practical work.	• To be able to identify risks and carry out practical work safely.	• Learners know the risks and work safely doing practical work.
4TWSc.06 Carry out practical work safely.	• To be able to identify risks and carry out practical work safely.	• Learners know the risks and work safely doing practical work.

LANGUAGE SUPPORT

The two key words for this topic are:
- **conductor** – a material that allows electricity to pass through it
- **insulator** – a material that does not allow electricity to pass through it

You will be using the words over and over again throughout this topic and following topics.

At some point in Science, learners will come across these same words in connection with heat.

In English the word 'conductor' is also the name for a person who leads an orchestra or who checks tickets on a train.

Since it is two years since learners did Electricity, it will be a good idea to revise the words introduced in Stage 2:
- **component** – a part
- **circuit** – a pathway where electric current flows round
- **cell** – a source of energy or power for a circuit
- **connecting wire** – the plastic covered copper wire that connects all the components of the circuit
- **lamp** – the lamp that lights up in a circuit
- **lamp holder** – the base the lamp or lamp is fixed in

Common misconceptions

Misconception	How to identify	How to overcome
The cell makes the electricity which then flows around the circuit.	Ask learners what the cell is doing in the circuit. If they say the cell makes the electricity they have the misconception.	You will have to tell them that the electricity is inside the copper wires (free electrons) and the energy in the cell pushes the electricity round the circuit.
Electricity can only come from the mains.	Ask learners where the electricity comes from to light the lamp in the circuit. If they say the same place as the light switch for the classroom or mains supply they have the misconception.	Learners can see that the electricity is in the circuit and not coming from a mains supply.
Why can't the wire stop at the lamp? Why does it need to go back to the cell?	Ask learners if they think the circuit can end at the lamp. If they say yes they have the misconception.	This misconception is linked with the first one. Learners think that the electricity is generated by the cell. But the electricity is inside the copper wires and it needs to be pushed round the circuit by the cell and there needs to be a continuous path from one end of the cell to the other.

Starter ideas

1 You've gotta have a circuit (5–10 minutes)

Resources: Components for a simple circuit – lamp, wires, switch, cell; Digital Classroom song: You've got to have a circuit (optional)

Description: Build a simple circuit. Turn on the switch and the lamp lights up. Ask learners what this is (a circuit). What is causing the light to come on? (Electricity).

This activity is very good for overcoming misconception 3.

⟩ **Digital Classroom:** If you have access to the Digital Classroom component, play the song 'You've got to have a circuit' at least twice. Learners will soon be joining in the song! The i button will explain how to use the song animation.

2 Getting started (5–10 minutes)

Resources: Learner's Book; connecting wire, lamp, lamp holder, cell

Description: Hold up each component in turn and ask learners to identify it on the diagram and say what it does in the circuit. (The numbers in the answers section refer to the numbers on the drawing of the circuit in the Learner's Book.)

Learners tell you what they think the cell is for. You can correct misconceptions 1 and 2 at this point.

Main teaching ideas

1 Think like a scientist: Test which materials conduct electricity (40 minutes)

Learning intentions: Use a fair test to group objects into conductors and insulators of electricity; make predictions and identify if results support, or do not support, predictions; describe simple patterns in results and make a conclusion from results; identify and explain risks and make sure they work safely with electricity.

Resources: Learner's Book. Digital Classroom activity: Which materials conduct electricity? (optional)

For this activity each group will need one 20 cm long piece of plastic covered wire with a crocodile clip on one end; a screwdriver; a 1.5 V cell in a cell holder with a crocodile clip on the end of one of the wires; a 1.5 V lamp in a lamp holder; a collection of at least six objects made of different materials, for example, a cork, a coin, a nail, a plastic spoon, a metal spoon, an eraser, a rubber band, a key, a wooden stick such as a chopstick, things made of glass such as a glass beaker, paper, cotton cloth.

Description: Before they make their circuit, ask the class questions 1–2. These questions are about safety and get them to think why they have to be careful.

Tell learners to prepare their prediction and results table before they start (see Learner's Book).

Then divide learners into groups (see 'Practical guidance' below). Give each group a box of components and let learners choose objects to test – make sure they choose at least two metal objects, other objects can be plastic, paper, glass or wood.

Make sure each group has at least three conducting materials (e.g. a coin, a nail and a metal spoon) and three insulating materials (such as plastic, cork, wooden stick, glass).

Then they must predict which materials will be conductors and insulators and fill in these predictions on a table like this, but with more rows depending on how many materials they test.

Material	Prediction		Result	
	conductor	insulator	conductor	insulator
1				
2				
3				

Step 1 – secure the bare end of the wire from the cell holder to a terminal on the lamp holder. Secure the bare end of the separate piece of wire to the other terminal on the lamp holder. This involves bending the bare wire into a tiny circle and then putting the circle over the screw hole and screwing the screw down with the screwdriver. This takes practice to do neatly and quickly – learners should remember this from Stage 2.

The circuit should now look like the second drawing in the Learner's Book.

Step 3 – check that the circuit works. Hold the crocodile clips together. If the lamp lights up the circuit works (and if you separate the clips and the lamp goes out).

What to do if the lamp does not light up: Learners will be very disappointed if their lamp does not light up. But tell them this is a common occurrence and they must find the fault and try again! Check:

• All the connections – is the tape holding the wire to the cell securely?

• Are the screws tight on the lamp holder?

Step 4 – when they are sure that the circuit works, they then test each material. Hold the crocodile clip of one wire at one end of the object. Hold the second crocodile clip at the other end. If the lamp does not light up you can try again to make sure.

Step 5 – Record results in the last two columns of the table.

Read the steps aloud in class. Make sure the learners understand what they must do. Walk round the groups all the time to check how they are getting on.

> **Practical guidance:** If possible, learners should do this activity themselves in groups. This way they will actually be achieving the success criteria themselves.

If it is not possible for the learners to do the activity, you should do it as a demonstration and involve learners in it as much as you can.

Some schools will have equipment to make circuits easily and other schools may have minimal supplies. In this course we have tried to show that even with the minimum equipment you can still do practical activities with a little bit of inventiveness. It is really important that all your learners have the experience of making their own circuits. This is the first circuit they will make in Stage 4. They should ideally work in pairs. But if equipment is limited divide the class into small groups. Supply each group or pair with a container (such as a box) to put their circuit equipment in. Make sure they label the box with their names. For the next few lessons they will need their box of circuit equipment.

In the equipment list, we have listed a cell in a cell holder and crocodile clips on the ends of some of the wires. Your school may not have access to these pieces of equipment but it is still possible to conduct this activity with your learners. You can secure the bare end of one piece of wire to the positive end of the cell with tape. Then secure the bare end of another piece of wire to the negative end of the cell with tape. The bare ends of the unconnected wires from the cell and lamp holder can then be placed on the objects the learners are testing. Just make sure that you touch only the plastic coated wire.

Safety warning: Depending on your learners' manual skills, you may decide that it is better for you to prepare the wires in advance, rather than ask learners to do this themselves. In that case, save one length of wire to demonstrate stripping the plastic away with wire strippers.

If learners strip the wires themselves, they must hold the wire firmly with one hand and use the other hand to hold the stripper. Teach the rule: always strip away from you!

You must tell students not to touch any bare electric wires. In fact, if they do touch the bare electric wire in a classroom activity using a 1.5V cell they might feel a tickle in their finger but will not get an electric shock. But it is important to make it a rule so that when they work with higher voltage electricity they will know it is important.

> **Digital Classroom:** If you have access to the Digital Classroom component, use the activity 'Which materials conduct electricity?' to consolidate learners understanding or assess their knowledge before moving onto the next topic. The i button will explain how to use the activity.

> **Differentiation ideas:** Ideally learners will work in small groups to do this activity. You can observe how they perform in a group situation. Some learners will want to organise, others will hang back and let others do the work. Encourage each member of the group to have a job to do, for example, one member can be responsible for placing the material to be tested for a certain number of seconds and another responsible for recording predictions and results.

If you have to do this activity as a demonstration, make sure you involve different learners to help you. Repeat each step so that different learners can help you each time.

> **Assessment ideas:** Learners can answer the Self-assessment questions in the Learner's Book.

As you walk around the class you can check how different groups are working together. This can give you ideas on what to change next time they do a group activity.

2 Workbook 6.1: Focus, Practice and Challenge exercises (10 minutes each)

Learning intention: To identify some common electrical insulators and conductors; describe simple patterns in results and make a conclusion from results

Resources: Workbook 6.1

Description: Learners answer questions in the Workbook (see 'Differentiation ideas' below).

> **Differentiation ideas:** The Focus exercise is the most straightforward exercise, where learners have to complete sentences and fill in a table.

In the Practice exercise, learners must recognise a conductor or an insulator in circuits and predict whether the lamp will come on or not.

In the Challenge exercise, learners must comment on an activity done by two learners, make predictions, make a conclusion and use their conclusion to classify other objects. They write their own sentence and fill in a table.

> **Assessment ideas:** Go through the answers in class at the beginning of your next lesson.

3 Worksheet 6.1, Help sheet and Stretch questions (10–15 minutes)

Learning intentions: To analyse data about how well different metals conduct electricity; draw a bar chart

Resources: Worksheet 6.1

Description: Learners read data supplied on the Worksheet, answer questions on the data and then draw a bar chart.

> **Differentiation ideas:** All learners can draw the bar chart. Learners who need more guidance with drawing a bar chart should use the Help sheet.

The Stretch questions are for learners who want an extra challenge to find out about semiconductors.

> **Assessment ideas:** Learners can assess their own bar chart by answering these questions (also in Worksheet pack):

Can I:	Very well	Most of the time	Not confident yet
decide what to put on each axis?			
label the axes correctly?			
decide on suitable scales on the axes?			
draw the bars accurately?			
label the bars neatly?			
give the bar chart a suitable heading?			

Plenary ideas

1 Workbook 6.1: Practice exercise (5–10 minutes)

Resources: Workbook 6.1

Description: A quick fun-to-do consolidation exercise to sum up what they have done in the topic

› **Assessment ideas:** Learners can mark each other's answers.

2 Compare results from different groups (5–10 minutes)

Resources: Results tables from different groups for the Think like a scientist activity

Description: Tell groups to report back to class the results they recorded from doing the Think like a scientist activity. Combine everyone's results in a table on the board

› **Reflection ideas:** Learners can ask themselves:

- How well did I work in the group?
- What did I contribute?
- Could I have done better?

CROSS-CURRICULAR LINKS

Main teaching idea 1 links with Technology.

Homework ideas

1 Learners can work through the Focus, Practice and Challenge exercises in the Workbook (see main teaching idea 2 for differentiation ideas). You could go through the answers to the exercises at the beginning of the next lesson. Learners can mark their own work or swap with a partner.

2 Learners complete Worksheet 6.1 (see main teaching idea 3 for differentiation ideas). This worksheet gives learners the chance to revise electrical conductors and draw a bar graph. You should take in the worksheets to check their work or let learners assess each other's work using the assessment grid provided for marking the bar chart.

Topic worksheets

Worksheet 6.1: Which materials conduct electricity?

In this topic, learners have found out that metals conduct electricity. However, not all metals conduct electricity to the same degree. Some are much better conductors of electricity than others. This worksheet gives data on this and learners answer questions on the data and then draw a bar chart. There is a Help sheet for less confident learners and a Stretch sheet to challenge more confident learners.

6.2 Does water conduct electricity?

LEARNING PLAN

Learning objectives	Learning intention	Success criteria
4Pe.04 Know some materials are good electrical conductors, especially metals, and some are good electrical insulators.	• To investigate if water conducts electricity.	• Learners can understand the difference between pure water and salty water and predict whether they conduct electricity.
4TWSp.03 Make a prediction describing some possible outcomes of an enquiry.	• To be able to make predictions and identify if results support predictions or do not support predictions.	• Learners can make predictions and identify if results support predictions or do not support predictions.
4TWSa.01 Identify whether results support, or do not support, a prediction.	• To be able to make predictions and identify if results support predictions or do not support predictions.	• Learners can make predictions and identify if results support predictions or do not support predictions.
4TWSc.01 Use observations and tests to sort, group and classify objects.	• To investigate if water conducts electricity.	• Learners test pure and salty water to see whether they conduct electricity.
4TWSa.03 Make a conclusion from results and relate it to the scientific question being investigated.	• To be able to make a conclusion from results.	• Learners test pure and salty water and make a conclusion from results.
4TWSp.05 Identify risks and explain how to stay safe during practical work.	• To be able to identify and explain risks and carry out practical work safely.	• Learners know the risks and work safely doing practical work.
4TWSc.06 Carry out practical work safely.	• To be able to identify and explain risks and carry out practical work safely.	• Learners know the risks and work safely doing practical work.

LANGUAGE SUPPORT

Key words for this topic are:

- **distilled water** – water that has been boiled and the steam has been allowed to cool down to form liquid water again. Distilled water has no salts dissolved in it and so it is pure water

- **pure water** – water with no salts dissolved in it

Point out that tap water, although it is impure from the point of view that it has salts dissolved in it (for example, chlorine to make it clean enough to drink), is safe for us to drink.

Learners may be aware of using distilled water to fill up a car cell.

Common misconceptions

Misconception	How to identify	How to overcome
Tap water is pure because it is safe to drink, or any clean water is pure. This can lead to thinking the water inside our bodies is pure.	Hold up a glass of water in class and ask learners if the water is pure. If they say yes they have the misconception.	The discussion in the Starter ideas and the Think like a scientist investigation in this topic should correct the misconception.

Starter ideas

1 Is this water pure? (5 minutes)

Resources: A glass of tap water

Description: Ask learners: Is this glass of tap water pure water?

If they say yes, you can explain that the water has salts dissolved in it, such as chlorine to purify it. So it is not pure in the sense that it contains other things. In Science, a pure substance is a substance that does not have anything added or mixed in it.

2 Where does the salt go? (5 minutes)

Resources: Glass of water and spoon of salt

Description: Ask learners to predict what will happen when you add the salt to the water and stir it. Demonstrate. Ask the learners what has happened to the salt. (It has dissolved.)

This demonstration shows learners that you often cannot see that water is not pure because it has salts dissolved in it. So it is difficult to assume that water is pure. The only way is to use distilled water. You will discuss this early in the lesson.

Main teaching ideas

1 Getting started (5 minutes)

Learning intention: To revise what they know already about dissolving and how to test to see if a material conducts electricity or not

Resources: Learner's Book

Description: Ask questions 1 and 2 in class. Learners should say that the salt disappears into the water – it dissolves. For question 2, learners should say that you make a circuit with a lamp and you put the object you want to test in the circuit and see if the lamp lights up or not.

2 Think like a scientist: Investigate whether water conducts electricity (30 minutes)

Learning intentions: To investigate if pure water and salty water conduct electricity; identify and explain risks and carry out practical work safely; make predictions and identify if results support, or do not support, predictions; make a conclusion from results.

Resources: Two 1.5 V cells in cell holders connected together with a crocodile clip on the end of one wire, a 1.5 V lamp in a lamp holder, one 20 cm length of plastic-coated electrical wire with a crocodile clip on one end, scissors or wire cutters, a sharp knife, or wire trimming tools two strips of aluminium foil 6 cm × 6 cm, 250 ml distilled water (available in litre bottles from supermarkets, hardware stores and car shops and garages), two teaspoons salt, a spoon or wooden spatula for stirring, a glass beaker or drinking glass; Digital Classroom Science Investigator video: Does water conduct electricity? (optional)

Description: Do this activity as a demonstration. Practise on your own first.

Discuss with the learners what you are doing at every step of the demonstration. Follow the instructions in the Learner's Book and in the 'Practical guidance' section below.

When you have finished the demonstration, tell learners to answer the questions in the Learner's Book in their notebooks.

> **Digital Classroom:** If you have access to the Digital Classroom component, use the Science Investigator video 'Does water conduct electricity?' to show the investigation being performed. It has prompts and pauses in the video to get your class to answer questions which appear on the screen.

You can show the video either before or after you do the investigation or at the end of the lesson. The i button will explain how to use the video.

> **Practical guidance:**

1   Cut the wire into a 20 cm length and strip off 2 cm of the plastic covering from the end of the wire that does not have a crocodile clip attached.

Safety warning: be careful when stripping the wire. Hold the wire firmly with one hand and use the other hand to hold the stripper. Always strip away from you.

This Think like a scientist activity is potentially even more dangerous than the one in Topic 6.1 (although the voltage is still low so would not cause a big electric shock). This is why we recommend you do this activity as a class demonstration. And be careful yourself!

2   Make a circuit with the 3 V cell, the lamp in the lamp holder and the length of wire.

3   Test the circuit by holding the crocodile clips together. If the lamp does not light up check all connections and try again.

4   Fold the two pieces of aluminium foil onto 2 cm wide strips and hold them in the crocodile clips. The reason you do this is to have a larger area of metal in contact with the water.

5   Pour 250 cm³ distilled water into the glass beaker.

Ask learners to predict at this point whether they think the lamp will light up when they dip the foil ends into the water.

6   Dip the aluminium foil ends into the distilled water. The lamp will not light up. Is this what they predicted?

7   Take the strips out of the distilled water. Add the salt to the water and stir it until has dissolved. Ask learners to predict at this point whether they think the lamp will light up when they dip the foil ends into the salt water.

8   Dip the aluminium foil ends into the salt water. The lamp will light up.

We have suggested using cells in cell holders and crocodile clips on the ends of some of the wires. Your school may not have access to these pieces of equipment but it is still possible to demonstrate this activity to your learners. You can connect the two cells together using tape. Make sure the two cells are held securely together. Use an elastic band wound round lengthways and perhaps wooden chopsticks or sate sticks to hold them in line as well as tape. You can then connect the bare ends of two pieces of wire to each end of the connected cells. Secure one wire to the lamp holder then connect a third piece of wire to the other side of the lamp holder. You can then press the aluminium foil onto the bare ends of the unconnected wires.

> **Assessment ideas:** All learners should be able to answer the first three questions with no difficulty. Questions 4, 5 and 6 need a bit more lateral thinking.

Go through answers in class. Learners can correct their own work.

3   **Workbook 6.2: Focus, Practice and Challenge exercises (10 minutes each)**

Learning intention: To understand the difference between pure water and salty water and predict whether they conduct electricity

Resources: Workbook 6.2

Description: Learners follow the instructions in the Workbook and write and draw their answers in the spaces provided.

> **Differentiation ideas:** The Focus exercise is a simple consolidation exercise where learners must recall the difference between pure water and tap water and the consequences for conducting electricity.

In the Practice exercise learners must design and draw a poster for a busy kitchen, warning workers not to handle electric stoves and appliances.

In the Challenge exercise learners read and answer questions about Jawad getting an electric shock. This exercise needs learners to analyse the situation and gives causes and effects.

> **Assessment ideas:** Go through answers at the beginning of your next lesson. Learners can correct their own work.

Plenary ideas

1 Reflection (5 minutes)

Resources: Learner's Book

Description: Now learners know their bodies conduct electricity, they can think about situations at home where they have to be careful with electricity.

> **Assessment ideas:** You could have a class discussion and ask learners to give you suggestions of dangerous situations.

2 Workbook 6.2: Focus exercise (5 minutes)

Resources: Workbook 6.2

Description: A short consolidation exercise. Learners answer questions in the Workbook.

> **Assessment ideas:** Go through answers in class

> **Reflection ideas:** Think about situations at home where you must be careful not to touch water and electricity

CROSS-CURRICULAR LINKS
Main teaching ideas 1, 2 and 3 link with Life Skills.

Homework ideas

1 Learners can complete the Practice exercise in the Workbook. Learners have to design and draw a poster using their knowledge about water conducting electricity. (see main teaching idea 3). Learners can use the assessment grid to self-assess or peer assess their poster.

2 Learners can move onto the Challenge exercise in the Workbook. This is a more difficult exercise where learners have to apply their knowledge to different situations.

6.3 Using conductors and insulators in electrical appliances

LEARNING PLAN

Learning objectives	Learning intention	Success criteria
4Pe.04 Know some materials are good electrical conductors, especially metals, and some are good electrical insulators.	• To be able to classify materials used in electrical appliances as electrical conductors or insulators.	• Learners can classify materials used in electrical appliances as electrical conductors or insulators.
4TWSc.01 Use observations and tests to sort, group and classify objects.	• To be able to classify materials used in electrical appliances and classify them as electrical conductors or insulators.	• Learners can classify materials used in electrical appliances using their knowledge of conductors and insulators.
4TWSc.06 Carry out practical work safely.	• To see how to use electrical appliances safely.	• Learners can understand how insulators help us to use mains electricity safely.
4TWSp.05 Identify risks and explain how to stay safe during practical work.	• To be able to predict whether appliances are being used safely or not.	• Learners can understand how insulators help us to use mains electricity safely.
4TWSa.04 Present and interpret results using tables, bar charts and dot plots.	• To be able to draw a dot plot to present results.	• Learners can draw a dot plot to present their results.

LANGUAGE SUPPORT

In this topic you will introduce words that learners may have come across if they use electricity at home.

- **cable** – a rope of wires
- **cord** – the plastic-coated wire that connects to a plug at one end and an appliance at the other end
- **electric shock** – the effect of a sudden flow of electricity through a person's body. A person's heart can be badly affected and the person can have a heart attack and die
- **mains electricity** – high voltage electricity that is sent to homes, schools, factories and offices to provide power for machines, lighting and appliances

- **plug** – a device for connecting an electric wire or cable to an electricity supply
- **pylon** – the structure that carries cables from the power station where electricity is made (or generated) to cities, towns and villages
- **volt** – a unit to measure the strength of electricity
- **voltage** – the measure of power of electricity. Mains electricity has a voltage of 110V in some countries and 220V in other countries. Check what it is in your country. This voltage is much higher than the voltage you are using in class for science experiments. Then you are using 1.5V cells
- **wall socket** – a hole in the wall connecting the plug on an appliance with the electric cables in the wall

Common misconceptions

Misconception	How to identify	How to overcome
The electricity we use in a circuit in class is the same as the electricity I use at home.	Ask learners question 3 in the 'Getting started' exercise at the start of the lesson: Do these appliances use the same electricity as the circuit we made in class? If they answer yes they have the misconception.	Explain at the start of the lesson about the difference in voltage.

Starter ideas

1 Getting started (5 minutes)

Resources: Pictures in the Learner's Book

Description: Discuss the pictures in class. Ask learners the questions in the Learner's Book.

2 How can I use this? (5 minutes)

Resources: Bring an electric kettle (or other electrical appliance such as a hair drier or electric drill) with a cord and plug to class.

Description: Demonstrate how you use e.g. the kettle: fill with water, plug into wall socket, switch on – water boils, kettle switches off, turn off at wall socket.

Ask learners the question: Does this appliance use the same electricity as the circuit we made in class? If they say yes, they have the misconception. They

may say no, they think it is stronger, which is a good answer. You will go on to explain voltage at the beginning of the lesson.

Main teaching ideas

In this topic you will be stressing safe usage of appliances which is very important when the voltage is high.

Remember from the last topic that our bodies contain lots of salty water which is a good conductor of electricity.

1 Activity 1: Classify materials used in electrical appliances as electrical conductors or insulators (20–30 minutes)

Learning intentions: To explain the difference between mains electricity and electricity we use in circuits in class; classify materials used in electrical appliances as electrical conductors or insulators; see how to use electrical appliances safely.

Resources: Learner's Book. You also need a cell for making a circuit, and the appliance you had in the starter activity to demonstrate with, as well as electric wall sockets, plugs and cables in the classroom.

Description: There is a lot of new vocabulary in this section. Before learners do the activity, read through the text in the Learner's Book. When reading the first paragraph show learners the cell they used to make their circuit in class. This is 1.5 volts. Here they learn the new words volt (or V for short) and voltage.

In the third paragraph you introduce mains electricity. They may be surprised at how much stronger it is than cells. Refer back to the starter activity and point out that electricity is the same but the strength or voltage is different. Hold up the electrical appliance and point out that this appliance (from starter activity 2) uses 110V or 220V electricity (according to what is used in your country).

Now it is essential that learners are very careful not to touch any bare electric wires. If they do they will get an electric shock, especially if their fingers are damp or sweaty. This is where safety rules really come into operation and it is where learners must be careful at home as well as at school.

Ask who has seen a pylon like the one in the photograph carrying cables (very thick cords containing copper wires) from the place where electricity is made (power station) to cities, towns and villages. Explain that the voltage in these cables is thousands of volts, and that before it gets to our homes the voltage has to be reduced to 110V or 220V or whatever voltage used in the country. (This is done at a 'step down' centre.)

When you read out the penultimate paragraph you can demonstrate by showing learners a wall socket on the wall and a plug and point out the metal parts and the plastic parts. Notice that the wall socket is made of plastic, which is an insulator. The wires, which are conductors, are <u>inside</u> the wall so we can't touch them.

Demonstrate with the appliance (e.g. an electric kettle) that the handle and outside is made of plastic which is an insulator. The inside is made of insulating material too. The electric wiring is inside surrounded by insulating plastic.

Then learners answer the questions in Activity 1 to consolidate what they have learnt.

Question 6 in Activity 1 involves learners counting electrical appliances in different rooms of their home and presenting results in a dot plot. Remind learners that the instructions for drawing a dot plot are at the end of the Learner's Book.

› **Differentiation ideas:** All learners should be able to answer these questions. For question 5, tell learners they do not need to draw a perfect picture of an appliance. The important thing is to label it correctly.

› **Assessment ideas:** Learners can answer questions in class and then you can go through their answers before moving on to the next section.

2 Activity 2: Predict safe or unsafe use of appliances (15 minutes)

Learning intentions: To identify dangerous use of electrical appliances; see how to use electrical appliances safely.

Resources: Learner's Book text and pictures.

Description: Learners were introduced to electric shocks in the previous topic. In this topic you focus on safe usage of appliances to avoid getting an electric shock.

Stress that all appliances are made to be safe to use. It is only when we use them incorrectly or do not replace damaged electric cords or plugs that they can become unsafe, especially when there is water around.

Discuss the examples in the Learner's Book of the worn cable and two ways in which a cable can become worn (these appear just before the activity).

Then learners can do Activity 2 in class. You can either get them to write their answers or discuss them in class or discuss first and then get them to consolidate by writing them in their notebooks.

› **Differentiation ideas:** For question 2 learners have to complete sentences but in question 3 they have to write their own sentences.

› **Assessment ideas:** Go through answers in class.

3 Workbook 6.3: Focus, Practice and Challenge exercises (10 minutes each)

Learning intentions: To identify electrical conductors and insulators in electrical appliances; to know how to use electrical appliances safely.

Resources: Workbook 6.3

Description: Learners write their answers in the Workbook.

> **Differentiation ideas:** The Focus exercise is a very simple exercise where learners identify electrical conductors.

In the Practice exercise learners have to apply their knowledge to a new situation and write sentences using key vocabulary.

The Challenge exercise is a bit more difficult. It contains a story about two boys who fly a kite that gets caught on the electricity pylons. Should they climb the pylon to get their kite?

> **Assessment ideas:** Check answers at the start of your next lesson.

Plenary ideas

1 What is the difference between a cell and mains electricity? (5 minutes)

Resources: Learner's Book, Digital Classroom song: There's electricity (optional)

Description: This is a self-assessment exercise. Learners must think about how they would tell a member of their family the difference between a cell (like a cell for a flashlight) and mains electricity. Learners could discuss this in pairs or small groups and you could compare ideas.

> **Digital Classroom:** If you have access to the Digital Classroom component, use the song 'There's electricity' to recap this topic before learners start on the self-assessment exercise. The i button will explain how to use the song.

> **Reflection ideas:** See Learner's Book

2 Workbook 6.3: Focus exercise (10 minutes)

Resources: Workbook 6.3

Description: See main teaching idea 3

> **Assessment ideas:** Check answers in class.

CROSS-CURRICULAR LINKS

Main teaching ideas 1, 2 and 3 link to Life Skills (safe use of electrical appliances).

Homework ideas

1 Learners can answer question 6 of Activity 1 while at home and draw a dot plot using their data.

2 Learners can work through the Workbook 6.3: Focus, Practice and Challenge exercises (see main teaching idea 3 for differentiation ideas). Go through the answers to the exercises at the beginning of the next lesson.

3 Learners complete Worksheet 6.3A, 6.3B or 6.3C (see the next section).

Topic worksheets

Worksheet 6.3A

Learners have to label electrical conductors and insulators on a picture of an electric plug.

Worksheet 6.3B

Learners draw and label their own electric plug.

Worksheet 6.3C

This is a more challenging task – learners identify electrical conductors and insulators on a picture of a lamp.

6.4 Switches

Learning objectives	Learning intention	Success criteria
4Pe.01 Know that an electrical device will not work if there is a break in the circuit.	• To see that an electrical device will not work if there is a break in the circuit.	• Learners see that a lamp will not light up if there is a break in the circuit.
4Pe.02 Describe how a simple switch is used to open and close a circuit.	• To be able to describe how a simple switch is used to open and close a circuit.	• Learners can describe how a simple switch is used to open and close a circuit.
4Pe.04 Know some materials are good electrical conductors, especially metals, and some are good electrical insulators.	• To choose equipment to carry out an investigation and use it appropriately.	• Learners can use knowledge of conductors and insulators to choose materials to make a simple switch.
4TWSc.03 Choose equipment from a provided selection and use it appropriately.	• To choose equipment to carry out an investigation and use it appropriately.	• Learners can use knowledge of conductors and insulators to choose materials to make a simple switch.
4TWSp.05 Identify risks and explain how to stay safe during practical work.	• To be able to identify risks and carry out practical work safely.	• Learners know the risks and work safely doing practical work.
4TWSc.06 Carry out practical work safely.	• To be able to identify risks and carry out practical work safely.	• Learners know the risks and work safely doing practical work.
4TWSp.03 Make a prediction describing some possible outcomes of an enquiry.	• To be able to make a prediction and test our prediction to see if it is correct.	• Learners can make a prediction and test their prediction to see if it is correct.
4TWSa.01 Identify whether results support, or do not support, a prediction.	• To be able to make a prediction and test our prediction to see if it is correct.	• Learners see that a lamp will not light up if there is a break in the circuit.
4TWSa.03 Make a conclusion from results and relate it to the scientific question being investigated.	• To be able to make a conclusion from results.	• Learners can conclude that a circuit is complete when the switch is closed.

LANGUAGE SUPPORT

The only new word is:

• **switch** – a device for closing or opening a circuit

We also use this word as a verb in English, for example 'switch on the light please.'

As a verb, switch can also mean change in English. For example: 'I'm going to switch classes' (meaning I'm going to change classes).

Starter ideas

1 Getting started (5 minutes)

Resources: Picture in Learner's Book

Description: Look at the picture and ask class questions 1–3.

2 What electrical appliances do you have at home? (5 minutes)

Resources: Look back to pictures of appliances in Topic 6.3 in the Learner's Book.

Description: Ask class: How do you turn on the microwave? How do you turn it off? (You use a switch.)

Main teaching ideas

1 Think like a scientist 1: Make a switch (30 minutes)

Learning intentions: Know which materials are electrical conductors and which are electrical insulators; choose suitable materials to make a simple switch to open and close a circuit; see that an electrical device will not work if there is a break in the circuit; identify risks and carry out practical work safely; make predictions and see if results support the predictions or not.

Resources: Learner's Book. Each pair or group will need:

• a small block of wood or hardboard, about 5 cm × 2 cm

• two drawing pins

• wire – 2 pieces 15 cm each

• a sharp knife or wire trimming tools

• a metal paper clip, not plastic coated.

> **Practical guidance:** Be careful when using the knife. Learners should only use the knife when you are there to help them. Alternatively they could use wire trimming tools.

Description: Follow the illustrated instructions in the Learner's Book.

When learners have finished making their switch, tell them to the answer questions on choosing materials for the switch in their notebooks.

2 Think like a scientist 2: Make a circuit with a switch (20 minutes)

Learning intentions: Describe how a simple switch is used to open and close a circuit; make a prediction and test to see if your prediction is correct.

Resources: Learner's Book. Each pair or group will need:

• the switch they have made in the previous activity

• the components in their box: a cell in a cell holder, a lamp in a lamp holder, a 30 cm piece of wire, a sharp knife or wire trimming tools, scissors

• a plastic or wooden chopstick.

Description: Learners should work with the same partner or group as in the previous activity.

Learners must make their circuit as they did in Topic 6.1, but this time include a switch. To do this they will need the extra piece of wire cut in half and the ends bared.

Once they have finished making the circuit, they should predict what will happen when they close the switch. Observe the lamp. It should light up.

When learners have finished making and testing their circuit tell them to answer the questions in their notebooks.

> **Practical guidance:** What to do if the bulb does not light up: check all the connections – is the tape holding down the wire securely?

Depending on your learners' manual skills, you may decide that it is better for you to prepare the wires in advance, rather than ask learners to do this themselves. In that case, save one length of wire to demonstrate stripping the plastic away.

If learners strip the wires themselves, make sure they use a wire stripper. They must hold the wire firmly with one hand and use the other hand to hold the stripper. Always strip away from you!

Switches are a safety measure in a way because if the switch is OFF there is no current flowing and you can't get a shock. So you can add to your safety rules:

• Always turn the switch OFF when not using an electrical appliance.

We have suggested using a cell in a cell holder but if your school does not have access to this piece of equipment, the learners can tape the wires to either end of the cell.

> Assessment ideas: Peer assessment (Learner's Book). Learners answer questions on how well their partner did in the activity.

3 Workbook 6.4: Focus, Practice and Challenge exercises (10 minutes each)

Learning intention: To describe how a simple switch is used to open and close a circuit.

What idea is good for: Consolidation

Resources: Workbook 6.4

Description: Learners answer questions in the Workbook

> Differentiation ideas: The Focus exercise has questions on a similar circuit to the one the learners have made. The Practice and Challenge exercises use circuits with different components and a second picture of an iron using mains electricity, so learners will need to use the same concept of a switch closing or breaking a circuit and relate it to different situations.

> Assessment ideas: Go through answers in class. Get learners to mark their own work or swap with a partner.

Plenary ideas

1 You've gotta have a circuit (5 minutes)

Resources: Digital Classroom song: You've gotta have a circuit

Description: If you have access to the Digital Classroom component, this is a catchy song that the learners have heard in earlier stages, but it is very

relevant to this topic. The i button will explain how to use this song animation.

2 Workbook 6.4: Focus exercise (5–10 minutes)

Resources: Workbook 6.4

Description: An easy consolidation exercise which all learners can do. Learners write answers in the Workbook.

CROSS-CURRICULAR LINKS

Main teaching ideas 1, 2 and 3 link with Technology.

Homework ideas

1 Learners can work through the Focus, Practice and Challenge exercises in the Workbook (see main teaching idea 3 for differentiation ideas). Go through the answers to the exercises at the beginning of the next lesson. Learners can mark their own work or swap with a partner.

2 Learners complete Worksheet 6.4A, 6.4B or 6.4C. See below for differentiation ideas. These worksheets give learners the chance to choose different suitable materials to make a switch. In Worksheets 6.4B and 6.4C they can make their own switch out of easily available materials at home.

Encourage learners to make switches and bring them to the next lesson. You can try their switches out in a circuit.

Topic worksheets

Worksheet 6.4A

This worksheet has questions on a switch, which is the same as the one the learners have already made, with an extra question asking for suggestions of alternative materials which could have been used.

Worksheet 6.4B

This worksheet gives pictures of a completely different switch made of coins and cardboard which learners have to analyse, and, in question 3, make if they want to.

Worksheet 6.4C

This worksheet shows learners how to make a switch out of a clothes peg and has questions about how it will work.

6.5 Changing the number of components in a circuit

LEARNING PLAN

Learning objectives	Learning intention	Success criteria
4Pe.03 Describe how changing the number or type of components in a series circuit can make a lamp brighter or dimmer.	• To investigate how changing the number or type of components in a circuit make a lamp shine more brightly or less brightly.	• Learners can change the number of lamps or cells in a circuit and observe how this affects the brightness of the lamps.
4TWSp.03 Make a prediction describing some possible outcomes of an enquiry.	• To be able to make predictions and identify if results support predictions or do not support predictions.	• Learners can make predictions and see if results support their prediction.
4TWSa.01 Identify whether results support, or do not support, a prediction.	• To be able to make predictions and identify if results support predictions or do not support predictions.	• Learners can make predictions and see if results support their prediction.
4TWSa.02 Describe simple patterns in results.	• To be able to describe simple patterns in results and make a conclusion from results.	• Learners can identify a pattern in results and make a conclusion.
4TWSa.03 Make a conclusion from results and relate it to the scientific question being investigated.	• To be able to describe simple patterns in results and make a conclusion from results.	• Learners can identify a pattern in results and make a conclusion.
4TWSp.05 Identify risks and explain how to stay safe during practical work.	• To be able to identify risks and carry out practical work safely.	• Learners know the risks and work safely doing practical work.
4TWSc.06 Carry out practical work safely.	• To be able to identify risks and carry out practical work safely.	• Learners know the risks and work safely doing practical work.

LANGUAGE SUPPORT

We introduce the word 'cell' in this topic.

• **battery** – a source of energy made up of more than one cell which pushes electricity around a circuit

The batteries we use in school experiments usually have 3V or 4.5V or 6V and later 12V. From a safety point of view, this voltage is not going to cause a big electric shock if a learner touches

bare wires – they may feel a prickle. However, it is good to make sure they do take care not to touch a bare wire to prepare them for using appliances at home, which are high voltage, safely.

• **brightly** (adverb) – shines with a stronger light

• **brightness** (noun) – how strong the light shines

• **dimly** (adverb) – shines with a weaker light

Starter ideas

1 Getting started (5 minutes)

Resources: Learner's Book

Description: Learners answer the questions in the Learner's Book. For question 1, you could hold up the various components for learners to name and say what they are for.

2 Batteries (5 minutes)

Resources: Learner's Book; a 1.5 V cell, a 3 V cell, a selection of batteries used for flashlights, cell phones, toys. Show learners the voltage of each one.

Description: Read the section under 'Cells and batteries' in the Learner's Book. Hand out the different batteries for learners to pass around. An 'AA' cell is 1.5 V. Flashlights use batteries use between 3.5 V to 8 V batteries. A cell phone uses a 3.7 V cell.

Ask learners how big the cell is in a car. (A 12 V cell.)

Main teaching ideas

1 Think like a scientist: What happens when we change the number of components in a circuit? (30–60 minutes depending on whether you do the main activity as a demonstration or groups do the activity themselves, or both.)

Learning intentions: Investigate how changing the number or type of components in a circuit make a lamp shine more brightly or less brightly; be aware of safety and work safely in practical work; make a prediction and see if results support, or do not support, a prediction; describe simple patterns in results and make a conclusion from results.

Resources: Learner's Book; the switch that learners have made in Topic 6.4; the following components (they will need to add to their box): two 1.5 V cells in cell holders, three lamps in lamp holders, a screwdriver, a 180 cm piece of wire, a sharp knife or wire trimming tools, scissors, wooden chopsticks or ice lolly sticks, sticky tape.

Description: Learners should work with a partner or group. If you do not have enough resources, you can do a demonstration, but make sure you ask learners

to come and help you so that they can experience actually making the circuit.

It would be a good idea to demonstrate first and then let the learners work in their group. You can include a circuit with three cells and only one lamp in a circuit in your demonstration – the lamp will pop, but at least you have only wasted one lamp!

Tell learners to make their own table to record predictions and results, as shown in the Learner's Book.

You could also show the video of this activity before the learners do it for themselves (see main teaching idea 2).

At the end of the practical work tell learners to answer the Learner's Book questions in their notebooks.

› **Practical guidance:** Follow these steps:

1 Join two cells together to make a 3V cell. Make sure the positive and negative terminals are connected to each other.

2 Cut the wire into 15 cm lengths. Bare the ends of the wire using wire strippers or a sharp knife.

3 Connect up the circuit with three lamps in lamp holders and a switch as shown in the picture in the Learner's Book.

4 Check that the circuit is complete when you close the switch. If not, check your connections.

5 Close the switch. Observe the brightness of the lamps. Now you are going to change the number of lamps.

6 Open the switch. Remove one of the lamps in a holder. Reconnect the circuit. Predict whether the lamps will be brighter or dimmer when you close the switch.

7 Close the switch. Observe the lamps. Check your prediction. Now you are going to change the number of cells in your circuit.

8 Make a circuit with three cells and three lamps in lamp holders. Close the switch. Observe how brightly the lamps are shining.

9 Now open the switch. Remove one of the cells so that there are two cells left. Predict how bright the lamps will be when you close the switch.

10 Close the switch. Test your prediction.

This work requires a sharp knife. Depending on your learners' skills, you may decide it is better to prepare the wires in advance, rather than ask learners to do it themselves. If they do it themselves, demonstrate with one piece of wire, stripping the plastic away from you. Do this on a hard, non-slip surface. You could use several layers of newspaper or old magazine to cut on.

Learners should wait until you are there to help them before using the knife. Alternatively, they could use wire trimming tools.

Do not touch the bare wires if the circuit is closed.

Re-enforce the safety rules you have already covered.

We have suggested using cells in cell holders but your school may not access to these pieces of equipment. In this case, the learners can tape the cells together. To make sure you have a firm connection it is a good idea to cut two pieces of a wooden chopstick or ice lolly stick to the length of the two batteries. Then tape together with sticky tape. You can also wind an elastic band around the batteries lengthways to make a firmer hold. The learners can then tape the ends of the wires to either end of the connected cells.

⟩ **Assessment ideas:** Assess learners as you walk around the class, checking on how they are getting along with their circuits. You could use this checklist.

Is the learner:

- contributing to the group work?
- listening to others?
- taking the lead or happy to watch others?

Learners can assess each other's circuit building skills using the peer assessment in the Learner's Book.

2 **Digital Classroom Science Investigator video: What happens when we change the number of components in a circuit? (10 minutes)**

Learning intentions: Investigate how changing the number or type of components in a circuit make a lamp shine more brightly or less brightly; be aware of safety and work safely in practical work; make a prediction and see if results support, or do not support, a prediction; describe simple patterns in results and make a conclusion from results.

Resources: Digital Classroom Science Investigator video: What happens when we change the number of components in a circuit?

Description: The video shows two Stage 4 learners doing the Think like a scientist investigation and has pauses with questions such as 'Predict what will happen when...'

Show the video and pause when there is a question on the screen. Tell learners to answer the question. Then continue with the video. The i button will explain how to use the Science Investigator video.

⟩ **Differentiation ideas:** This could help learners who struggle with the practical work. The video shows two Class 4 learners doing the Think like a scientist 1 activity.

3 **Workbook 6.5: Focus, Practice and Challenge exercises (10 minutes each)**

Learning intention: Describe how changing the number or type of components in a series circuit can make a lamp brighter or dimmer; know that an electrical device will not work if there is a break in the circuit.

Resources: Workbook 6.5

Description: Learners follow instructions and write their answers in the Workbook.

⟩ **Differentiation ideas:** All three exercises offer consolidation of the topic. The Focus exercise is a very straightforward activity. The Practice exercise is a little more demanding. The Challenge exercise includes questions on how to make the circuit as well as adding and taking away components.

⟩ **Assessment ideas:** Go through answers at the beginning of your next lesson. Learners can mark their own or each other's work.

Plenary ideas

1 **Digital Classroom Science Investigator video: What happens when we change the number of components in a circuit? (10 minutes)**

Resources: Digital classroom Science Investigator video: What happens when we change the number of components in a circuit?

Description: See main teaching idea 2.

2 **Peer assessment (2 minutes)**

Resources: Assessment grid in the Learner's Book

Description: Learners can rate each other's skills of connecting components of a circuit and adding or taking away components. They also compare their skill now with earlier attempts at building a circuit.

> **Reflection ideas:** According to how their partner rated them, learners can think about how they could improve further.

CROSS-CURRICULAR LINKS

Main teaching ideas 1 and 2 link to Design and Technology.

Homework ideas

1   Learners work through the Focus or Practice exercise in the Workbook. These exercises are straightforward consolidation exercises.

2   Learners can move onto the Challenge exercise in the Workbook. In this exercise learners recall how to build and change the circuit as well as predicting results. Go through homework answers in class at the beginning of your next lesson.

PROJECT: BATTERIES

4SIC.01 Describe how scientific knowledge and understanding changes over time though the use of evidence gained by enquiry

4TWSc.07 Use secondary information sources to research an answer to a question

All the circuits you and the learners have made in this unit have included a cell. These batteries contain chemical substances that react together. This reaction supplies energy. The energy pushes the electricity round the circuit. How did scientists make this discovery? How did scientific ideas about batteries change over time?

The beginning of the story is in the Learner's Book. Read the story to the learners about the Baghdad cell and Galvani's discovery. Then move on to Volta's voltaic pile. Take note that Volta repeated Galvani's experiment many times using different materials – he was looking for more evidence. This evidence led him to the important discovery that it was the reaction between two different metals that produced the electricity. This idea is still used today.

Ask learners where they think the term 'volt' for strength of electricity comes from. The answer is Alessandro Volta.

The task for learners is to continue this story of how batteries were invented by doing some research on Alessandro Volta's voltaic pile.

Learners can use library books or the internet to find out how Alessandro Volta's cell worked.

Assessment for presentation

Learners should present their work on a sheet of A4 paper. They should include drawings or diagrams.

You can assess learners' projects using these guidelines:

How well did learner find information?

How well did learner choose what to write?

Did learner choose good illustrations?

Did learner manage to fit project on an A4 page?

How well did learner present their work?

> Glossary

absorb – to take in a substance. For example, if you spill a liquid you can pat it with a paper towel. The paper towel absorbs the liquid

anticlockwise – the opposite of clockwise which is the direction the hands of the clock move

apparent movement – the movement does not really happen but it looks like it happens

ash – burnt material. For example, the grey powdery material left when wood has burnt

asteroid – a rocky mass that orbits the sun. These are similar to planets but much smaller

axis – anything that spins or rotates has to turn around a central line. This line is the axis

battery – a source of energy made up of more than one cell which pushes electricity around a circuit

beak – the part of a bird used to catch and hold food

bones – hard, strong parts inside our body that give our body shape and keep us upright

brightly (adverb) – shines with a stronger light

brightness (noun) – how strong the light shines

cable – a rope of wires

carnivore – an animal that eats other animals

change of state – when materials and substances change from one form to another when they are heated or cooled

chemical reaction – when we mix together two substances and they both change to make a new substance

closest – the one that is nearest. For example, The closest shop from my home is just down our road

coastal area – a low lying area along the border between land and sea. The coastline is the outline of the border between the land and the sea as you see it on a map

comet – a lump of ice and dirt which moves in a large orbit around the sun. Halley's comet (named after the astronomer Halley) takes 76 years to make one orbit around the sun

compare – to look at two or more things and say what is the same about them and what is different about them

composite volcano – a volcano that erupts lava and ash which builds up into a cone-shaped mountain. 'Composite' means being made up of more than one type of material

conclusion – what you have found out from an investigation

conductor – a material that allows electricity to pass through it

consumer – a living thing that cannot make its own food and obtains energy by eating other living things, usually an animal that eats plants or other animals

contract – when muscles get shorter and fatter. Muscles feel hard when they contract

cord – the plastic-coated wire that connects to a plug at one end and an appliance at the other end

core – the centre of the Earth. 'Core' is a commonly used word in English that always means 'at the centre of'. For example, the core of an apple is at the centre of the apple, the core ideas are the ideas most central to the topic

crack open – break something open. For example, you can use nut crackers to crack the shell off a nut

crater – a large hole at the top of a volcano where material erupts

crust – the outer layer of the Earth. Note that 'crust' is also used in English to describe the hard outer layer of bread

destroy – to make something not exist anymore, for example to destroy a letter by burning it

dimly (adverb) – shines with a weaker light

distilled water – water that has been boiled and the steam has been allowed to cool down to form liquid water again. Distilled water has no salts dissolved in it and so it is pure water

earthquake – a shaking of the Earth

electric appliances – machines that use electrical energy to make them work, for example an electric kettle

electric shock – the effect of a sudden flow of electricity through a person's body. A person's heart can be badly affected and the person can have a heart attack and die

electrical energy – the form of energy we get from electricity

energy – anything that can cause movement or carry out an action

energy transfer – when energy moves from one place to another place or from one object to another object

epicentre – the point on the surface of the Earth immediately above the focus. The epicentre is where the most damage occurs

erupt – a verb which means to shoot out suddenly. For example, if you boil milk in a saucepan and do not watch it, the milk can erupt out of the pan and on to the stove

exoskeleton – the hard skins or shells on the outside of the bodies of some invertebrates

external structure – materials that make up the surface of the Earth. 'External' means 'outside', so we are referring to materials on the surface of the Earth that we can see

focus – the point in the crust under the Earth's surface where the earthquake starts. We also use the word 'focus' in English to mean the central point. For example, the focus of the lesson was earthquakes

food chain – a drawing that shows the order in which animals eat plants and other animals to get energy

frame – something that gives support and shape from the inside

function – the job or use of something, for example the function of a pen is to write

furthest – the one that is the most far away

germs – very tiny living things that can cause diseases, for example we wash our hands before we eat so we don't get germs on our food

gills – an organ that fish have to allow them to breathe

globe – a model of the Earth. However, in everyday life you often hear people talking about the globe meaning the whole world

herbivore – an animal that eats plants

hip – the bone that joins the leg to the upper part of the body

identification key – a set of questions that allows us to name or group things

image – a picture of the object that you see on a screen or in a mirror

infect – when the germs get into your body and make you ill

infectious disease – a disease that is caused by germs

instructions – information that tells us how to do something, for example Ali has a set of instructions to tell him how to build a model car

insulator – a material that does not allow electricity to pass through it

internal structure – materials that make up the inside of the Earth. 'Internal' means 'inside' so we are referring to materials inside the Earth that we can't see

invertebrate – an animal that has a backbone or spine

jaw – the skull bone that moves when we eat or talk

landslide – a mass of rocks and soil that slides down a slope. The vibrations from the earthquake cause these to happen

lava – magma that reaches the surface of the Earth

length – how long something is; for example, the length of a ruler is 30 cm

magma – melted rocks

mains electricity – high voltage electricity that is sent to homes, schools, factories and offices to provide power for machines, lighting and appliances

mantle – the layer of the Earth below the crust which consists of magma

materials – kinds of matter that we use, such glass and metal

medicines – substances that we use to help us get better when we are ill, for example cough mixture helps us to stop coughing

melting – when a solid changes state to become a liquid

mirror – a very smooth, shiny surface that reflects light well

model – an object or drawing that helps us understand how something works or see what something looks like that we can't see in real life

muscles – parts of the body that are joined to bones and allow us to move

omnivore – an animal that eats plants and other animals

orbit – the movement of a body in space around a larger body in space. For example, the Earth moves around the sun in an orbit. The moon moves around the Earth in an orbit

organs – parts inside the body that do different jobs

particles – very tiny pieces of something

physical process – when a substance changes form, e.g. melts, but does not become a new substance

plateau – a flat uplifted area of rock. For example, most of India and Africa consists of a plateau

plug – a device for connecting an electric wire or cable to an electricity supply

pour – to make a liquid or other substance flow out of or into a container

powder – a solid with fine grains that have air spaces between them, such as baby powder or flour

predator – an animal that kills and eats other animals

predict – to say what you think will happen based on what you already know or have observed, for example we can predict that we will burn our hands if we touch a hot stove

prevent – to stop, for example a raincoat prevents us from getting wet when it rains

prey – an animal that a predator kills and eats

producer – a plant that makes its own food using energy from the Sun

proof – scientific evidence that something is true

property – what a substance or material is like, or the way it behaves

protect – keep safe from harm, for example, a jacket will protect you from the cold

prove – to find proof that something is true when doing a scientific investigation

pure water – water with no salts dissolved in it

pylon – the structure that carries cables from the power station where electricity is made (or generated) to cities, towns and villages

ray – a line that light travels in. We often talk about the Sun's rays

ray diagram – a diagram to show how light travels

react – this is when a substance changes when it is mixed with another substance

reflect – the action of light bouncing off a surface

reflection – when light bounces off a surface

relax – when muscles get longer and thinner. Muscles feel soft when they relax

rib cage – the bones of the chest

risk – the possibility of something happening. For example, if you climb a tree, there's a risk you might fall

rust – a reddish-brown powder that forms on some metals

secondary cone – a small volcano that erupts on the side of the main volcano

skeleton – the bones inside our body that are joined together to form a frame

skull – the bones of the head

solar system – the sun and the planets, moons, comets and asteroids which move around it. 'Solar' means sun

solidifying – when a liquid changes state to become a solid

source – where something comes from

spacecraft – a vehicle for travelling in space. For example, a space shuttle is a spacecraft which takes scientists to and from the space centre

spin – a verb that means to turn very fast. The best example of this is a spinning top

spine – the bones of the back

strain – to separate solids from the liquid they are in. For example, you use a strainer in the kitchen to separate solid foods from a liquid

substance – a particular type of solid, liquid or gas, for example water

support – to hold up something so that it doesn't fall down

surface – the top layer that is next to the air

switch – a device for closing or opening a circuit

tilted – at an angle, not vertical

transfers – changes into. For example, the energy of an earthquake transfers to waves

tsunami – a huge wave which happens when an earthquake starts under the sea

vaccinations – injections or other medicines that stop us from getting a disease

vent – a hole. For example, buildings have vents built into them to allow air in. The vents are grids with holes in

vertebrate – an animal that has a backbone or spine

volt – a unit to measure the strength of electricity

voltage – the measurement of the power of electricity. Mains electricity has a voltage of 110V in some countries and 220V in other countries. Check what it is in your country. This voltage is much higher than the voltage you are using in class for science experiments. Then you are using 1.5V cells

wall socket – a hole in the wall connecting the plug on an appliance with the electric cables in the wall

wave – a way in which energy travels. For example earthquakes travel through the Earth's crust in waves